test of faith

test of
faith

surviving my daughter's
life sentence

Bonnie S. Hirst

She Writes Press

Published September 2019
Printed in the United States of America
Print ISBN: 978-1-63152-594-0
E-ISBN: 978-1-63152-595-7
Library of Congress Control Number: 2019932269

For information, address:
She Writes Press
1569 Solano Ave #546
Berkeley, CA 94707

Cover and interior design by Tabitha Lahr

She Writes Press is a division of SparkPoint Studio, LLC.

ALL NAMES HAVE BEEN MODIFIED EXCEPT FOR THOSE OF FAMILY AND FRIENDS.

Versions of some pages were previously published in:
365 Ways to Connect with Your Soul—Safe, Protected, and Very Blessed
365 Ways to Connect with Your Soul—Taking Off the Blinders
Full Grown People—Toll Bridge Essay

Content taken from *Jesus Calling* by Sarah Young Copyright © 2004 by Sarah Young. Used by permission of Thomas Nelson.www.thomasnelson.com

To Lacey, may God continue to keep hope alive.

part 1

chapter 1

November 16, 2010

The jury has reached a verdict. My husband, Ron, our thirty-five-year-old daughter, Lacey, who is out on bail, and I are summoned to the third-floor courtroom.

Lacey's two-week jury trial is the culmination of nineteen months of grueling pretrial appearances. Flanked by her two lawyers, Lacey is at the table allocated for the defense. Behind her, Ron and I sit on a wooden bench, hips touching. Our friends surround us. The victim's family—haggard from watching their daughter's blood-speckled clothing presented as forensic evidence—gather to our left, behind the prosecutor. Spectators fill the remaining seats.

"All rise."

Reaching for Ron's work-callused hand, I interweave my slender fingers with his large ones; his warmth lessens my anxiety.

The jurors file in and stand next to their padded chairs. They make no eye contact. Judge Barlow enters in his black, flowing robe. As he takes his seat, I notice that the hefty legal publications he has referred to during the trial—which were always splayed open to the pages he wanted to quote—are now stacked in an orderly pile on the edge of his desk. The verdict is all that is left.

As we sit back down, Ron tucks our joined hands between us.

"Does the defendant wish to stand?" the judge asks. Lacey's chair scrapes across the floor. Her attorneys rise with her. Lacey's five-foot-four-inch figure looks like a divot between their towering frames. Her navy-and-white polyester blouse and black dress slacks communicate that she is a woman who should not be on trial for murder. Wire-rimmed glasses, short, tousled brown hair, and little to no makeup complete the image of who my daughter is.

Judge Barlow addresses the jury and asks to see the verdict paper. As he silently reads it, the pensive look on his face brings trepidation into my heart. Seldom has he shown emotion during this two-week trial, except for the times he pounded his gavel to quiet the courtroom.

He returns the paper to the jury foreman, who stands and clears his throat. My pulse quickens. I close my eyes and beseech God one last time, *Please, Lord, pronounce her innocent.*

The foreman reads the verdict. "We, the jury, find the defendant guilty of the crime of murder in the first degree."

My heart pounds with ravaging force; I feel its pulse throughout my body. My fingers clamp tight around Ron's knuckles.

The foreman continues. "We, the jury, find the defendant guilty of the crime of manslaughter in the first degree."

Ron's palm burns into mine with vise-like pressure. My lungs feel suspended.

"Count three, enhanced weapons charge: guilty."

The victim's family is jubilant. Fist pumps and loud, exhaled shouts of *"Yes!"* pierce the air. Ron and I, our hands riveted between us, clench one another torturously. Our stoic faces will deny the reporters their possible headline: "Parents Overwhelmed by Verdict."

Lacey turns tremulously away from the jury. I am unable to see her face. Her slim body reveals only a halo of the overweight young woman she was before our world began falling apart. The crestfallen slump of her sharp shoulder blades is a vision that will haunt me. With the verdict, guilty on all counts, the mandatory sentence will be life in prison without parole.

Courtroom activity fades into the background as I query myself: *Did I not pray correctly? Did I not believe enough in His power? Why has God forsaken my family and me?*

Uniformed police officers stand by the door as the courtroom empties.

Our friends, who have forged a protective bubble around us in court, congregate just outside the closed door. The judge and the jury have exited to their respective chambers. The room is vacant except for Ron, Lacey, her two lawyers, the two arresting officers, the lead investigator, and me. The officers appear stouter than they are in their dark blue uniforms and bulletproof vests. Their gleaming silver badges and matching nameplates seem overly flashy in the oppressive air. They block Ron and me from approaching Lacey by creating a barricade with their arms.

"We just want to hug her," I beg.

The officers hold their ground and shake their heads no.

Ron bristles beside me. "The hell we can't."

Matt, the lead investigator, intercedes on our behalf and nods a yes toward the officers. They drop their arms and they step aside. Gathering Lacey into my arms, I place a kiss on her cheek.

"Let's make this quick," demands one of the officers as he nudges me. "We need to get going."

Disengaging, I look into her shell-shocked eyes, and mine well up with tears. Lacey removes her wedding band, then her wristwatch, as the officers have instructed, and drops them into her open purse. Her hands shake as she lifts it toward me.

My chin quivers, and my mouth contorts as I try to hold in my disbelief. *Why, God?* This is not the scenario we envisioned. If we had received the not-guilty verdict, we were prepared to whisk Lacey away from the uproar that would assuredly have overtaken the courtroom.

It's Ron's turn. He folds her into his protective bear hug. The agony on his face shatters me, and I flee—out the courtroom doors, past our ever-vigilant friends, my head lowered so I can't see their faces or the sadness that would reflect from their eyes to mine. I bolt down the three flights of stairs and thrust open the side entrance door. Gasping for air in the isolated employees' courtyard, I collapse against a metal pole. My chest heaves as I bawl.

chapter 2

My belief in God was nurtured from a young age. Mom was a churchgoer, and we attended the local Presbyterian Church. My older sister, Patty, and I attended Sunday school, where the lessons centered on God answering prayers. In one Bible story, David prayed, and the Lord helped him conquer the giant soldier, Goliath. God protected David in his hour of need. My favorite story was about Daniel in the lion's den. Betrayed by jealous rivals, Daniel was condemned to death and thrown into a lair of hungry lions. Daniel called upon God to save him. The next day, when Daniel was lifted out of the den, no wound was found on him. He had trusted wholly in his Lord and had been protected.

I grew up believing that if I prayed the way David and Daniel did, God would answer my prayers also.

Each Sunday morning, Mom and Dad filled a blue enameled roasting pan with seasoned pot roast, potatoes, carrots, and onions and trusted it to bake while we were away. It did. The aroma of the braised beef that filled the house when we returned signified love, family, and home. Around our dinner table, we held hands and took turns saying grace. When Dad nodded to me that it was my turn, I recited my memorized verse: "Our gracious heavenly Father, we ask You to bless this food to the nourishment of our bodies. Amen."

The one other prayer I knew was, "Now I lay me down to sleep." I have a picture of my sister and me kneeling at the foot of our bed, our prayer hands touching our lips and our tiny toes peeking out from under our matching red-and-white-candy-striped pajamas.

We prayed at meals and bedtime, but our parents made no additional holy requirements of us, other than Sunday school.

Dad and Mom both worked for the Bureau of Reclamation, and we lived near hydroelectric dams. Our family spent weekends in the summer water skiing on the lake and in the winter zooming down the ski slope. The other fifty government families were the same as us: two parents, two children, one dog.

During my sixth-grade summer, I attended church camp. I can still see the luminosity of the campfire as the dancing light outlined my camp friends. Swaying together as if one body, we sang, "Kumbaya, My Lord." In translation, it means, "Come by here." On the last verse, I stretched my arms wide toward heaven, opened my heart, and invited God to enter my life. Warmth enveloped me. Unconditional love. Our singing flowed into "Michael Row the Boat Ashore." My heart filled with light, and I remember smiling and being joyful that I had bonded with God. From that moment forward, I knew He was with me. I knew I could rely on Him to answer my prayers.

As I entered junior high, I asked God for good grades and received mostly A's, some B's. I prayed to excel in the spelling bee, and my team won the countywide competition with the word *questionnaire*. My prayers in high school were petty, but they were answered: homecoming princess, debate team, and JV cheerleader. One prayer that wasn't granted was to become a varsity cheerleader, but I accepted God's inaction as a blessing, since I then applied and was chosen to be a Rotary exchange student to Denmark that year.

Ron and I were high school sweethearts and were married the summer I graduated. We moved to a little Mayberry-like town (pop. 1,000) and worked for Ron's dad at his full-service restaurant. I waitressed—a job I had enjoyed in high school—and learned the front-of-the-house operations of menu engineering, food costing, payroll, and balancing cash against sales. Ron set about mastering the busy restaurant kitchen.

After working side by side there for a couple of years, we moved on to other endeavors: cattle ranching, logging, and house building for Ron, and accounting for me. After our daughters, Lacey and Trilby, were born, we purchased a drive-in restaurant and soon established our little family in the small town.

When our girls were very young, they attended Sunday school at the Community Church. I don't know if they were taught the same Bible stories that had resonated with me. They never mentioned them, and I didn't ask. As I look back on their childhood, I regret not sharing my love of God with them. I guess I assumed they would come to know Him on their own, like I had. I did teach them to recite their evening prayer, though I don't remember having them kneel to pray, and rarely did we say grace before meals.

Eventually, they outgrew Sunday school, and I stopped attending church. In the evenings, I would wind their long, auburn hair onto pink foam rollers so the next day they would look appropriate to the world. I also often uttered the same words my dad had said to me growing up: "What will people think if you go to school looking a mess? What will people think if you wear that outfit? What will people think . . . ?"

Attempting to perpetuate the myth of the perfect mom, perfect family, I became the president of the PTA and helped garner enough community support to pass a much-needed school levy. Ron joined the Fraternal Order of the Eagles, the Elks, and the Jaycees. Our life appeared charmed. Our family activities more or less paralleled those of my childhood. We spent summers on the lake, basking in the sun, and in the winter, Ron and I taught our girls to snow ski. Camping with friends and maintaining forest trails on dirt bikes filled a lot of our weekends.

We attended high school volleyball, basketball, and football games. Lacey kept stats for the teams and was the tiger mascot her junior year. She worked at our drive-in and purchased her first vehicle at sixteen—an Isuzu pickup truck that she promptly decked out with pink and turquoise racing stripes.

Lacey enjoyed being self-sufficient, and her soft heart always stood up for the underdog. She was forever nurturing those down on their luck. Trilby, who was two years younger, participated and excelled in sports year-round. We cheered alongside other parents when the teams won and commiserated together when they lost. Our community was our stronghold, and we felt blessed to live where we did.

It seemed good things always came our way. I prayed, and God answered. I was confident that my prayers were the reason our life was not fraught with disaster. As I prayed, I'd become aware of God's presence. A calm would come over me when I talked with Him, and I felt His shroud of protection encapsulate me. I held my faith close, like a cherished memento.

I admire families that center their lives on God and His teachings, but that's not me. My life path is not splashy with sermon. I've never read a Bible front to back—although I own several—and I can't quote scripture, so I don't feel well-versed enough to share my faith with others. My most cherished Bible is my mother's well-used King James Version, with her name embedded in golden script on the front and her handwritten study notes in the margins. I love the heft of the open book upon my lap and the rustle of the onionskin pages as I thumb through them. Another prized keepsake is the pocketbook-size Bible my parents gave me when I was ten with my mom's graceful handwriting inside the cover: "To our precious daughter. May you come to know God's grace and abiding love. We love you so very much. Dad and Mom"

I often wonder: if I had been more vocal about my belief in God as our girls were growing up, would our lives be any different now?

I sat for the Enrolled Agent exam given by the IRS because I was operating my accounting business out of our home and felt the letters "EA" after my name would announce that I was well qualified to prepare tax returns. I studied for almost a year and asked God to help me succeed.

When the results arrived, my spirits soared. I had passed part one. Then it sank to the depths of a grave when I realized I flunked the second part. I hid the envelope in my top desk drawer and didn't tell anyone for over a week. That was my first adult failure, and I questioned why God hadn't come through for me. Was He telling me to dig deeper, that things aren't always easy?

The next test wasn't for another six months. There were study groups I could attend—but that would require asking for help. It's not in my nature to ask for help with anything.

The part I loved best about tax preparation and accounting was that there was always a solution. There was an answer to every dilemma. Sometimes it required lots of calculations, but I could always find an answer without asking a human being for help. I'm comfortable asking God for His assistance, but that's where it stops. To ask anyone else would mean I was incompetent.

I went back to studying and passed the next test. I proudly added the credentials to my advertising.

My bookshelves over the years have been filled with a variety of self-help books, from a handyman's fix-it guide to how to raise well-behaved children to herbal remedies for common illnesses. I even had an up-to-date *Encyclopedia Britannica* set before the internet became my preferred investigative tool. There was little I couldn't research and learn how to do—from troubleshooting printers, replacing toilet handles, and draining hot water tanks to calculating percentages to keep the restaurant viable and preparing my own financial statements. Every challenge was an opportunity to learn something new. Solving problems, to me, is like putting together a jigsaw puzzle. You spread the pieces out and then, as you find a place for each one, the picture begins to take shape. The answer forms. The delight of putting that final piece into place . . . superb.

chapter 3

Ron and I now owned two restaurants. We'd remodeled our drive-in to be full service, and from the success of its operation, we'd built a larger restaurant in a town nearby, thirty miles south. Two years prior to Lacey's verdict, I was at the larger restaurant, counting receipts, when Lacey arrived in tears.

Immediately, my mind went to my grandkids—Blaine, an intense yet sensitive eleven-year-old boy, and Meri, a frilly eight-year-old girl.

"Are the kids okay?" I demanded. "Has something happened to them?" In that flash of a second, I had them involved in an accident or diagnosed with some deadly illness.

"They're fine," Lacey said.

Closing the door, I reined in my fearful thoughts and handed her a tissue. "What's wrong, sweetie?"

"Danny is cheating on me. I've suspected something was going on, and he finally fessed up this morning."

I pictured Danny's lean build, his Ozzy Osbourne T-shirt, frayed jeans, and grease-stained fingernails.

"He's even brought her to our house. The kids know who she is."

"Oh, sweetheart," I said as I gathered her into a hug. Danny's job was to be Daddy Daycare, even though the kids weren't his. Lacey worked long hours, six days a week, as the finance manager for a growing car dealership. Danny had been in my grandkids' lives since they were very young and he loved them as his own.

I bit my tongue so I wouldn't lash out about him to Lacey. I'd already had a bad experience in that area. Lacey and her first husband had had a tumultuous marriage. When they fought, I had said unkind words about him, and then, when they made up, my comments had bounced like ricocheted bullets between Lacey, her husband, and me. This time I decided to keep my commentary to myself.

My daughter's tears dropped onto her jacket. "How could he bring her to my house?" She paused to blow her nose. "She's younger and skinnier and prettier than me."

Lacey had gained an alarming amount of weight that year. I imagined her looking into a mirror and feeling frumpy compared to this new woman in her husband's life.

"What's her name?" I asked.

"Selena Clark."

"Is she related to the Clarks in Oroville?" Our county is rural; we know most of the families in the area by name.

"Yeah, her mom lives there."

"How did Danny meet her?"

"I don't know, Mom. I just know he's screwing around. I'm not even sure how long it's been going on." Lacey received a text. After reading it, she called her boss to ask for the rest of the day off. "I'm headed home early," she said, standing to leave.

"It will all work out okay, sweetie," I said.

When I got home that evening, I opened my Women's Devotional Bible. It had pages where women shared stories of how God had helped them in their lives. I had highlighted many sections in the topic index—hope, faith, family, fear. Most times, though, I would just open it randomly and read the page that presented itself. It always felt meant to be when the comfort I was seeking miraculously appeared on the opened page.

After Danny's confession, not a week passed without Lacey stopping by my office several times. She always closed the door and chronicled her latest interaction with Danny. He had come home. He hadn't come home. He answered her texts. He didn't answer her texts. He let Selena drive the truck that Lacey had bought for him. He took Lacey's daughter with them. He left both kids home alone. Danny did this. Danny didn't do that. Her situation was disordering my life, and I worried about my grandchildren. I was angry with Danny for cheating and for being open about it with Blaine and Meri.

One day as I was heading home from work, I got my first glimpse of Selena. Danny was driving his silver Toyota pickup when our cars met on a straight stretch of Highway 97. His head was angled toward her, and he was touching the nape of her neck. In that glimpse of a second, with her leaning into Danny, a smile on her thin face and her hair slicked back into a ponytail, I was privy to their intimate moment.

Neither of them saw me, and I had the notion of following them. But I didn't. What good would it do? Things were obviously not getting better for Lacey, and entangling myself in Danny's affair was not going to help matters.

In the weeks to follow, many afternoons when I left the restaurant and drove north on the only road connecting the two small towns, I would see Danny driving away from his responsibilities, Selena by his side. I felt he needed to be at home to greet the kids when they got off the bus, ask them about their day, and get them a snack. He shouldn't be gallivanting all over the county with this new woman.

I became agitated and fretful that my grandkids were being left alone. Lacey had told me drugs were involved—I thought marijuana—and my mind jumped to all sorts of danger. If Blaine and Meri were home by themselves, what would keep someone from coming to the house and harming them? I had already told Lacey that I wasn't pleased that the kids were being left alone. She'd asked me to not interfere with Danny's parenting choices.

Please, Lord, keep my grandkids safe and give me guidance to know how and when to help them.

One day, I allowed my anxiety to get the better of me. I bought a cheap pair of small, foldable binoculars with camo print and drove to a spot across the river from Lacey's house. Playing the part of a private eye, I turned off my automatic headlights and dialed the radio volume down. I considered turning off the engine but decided against it, feeling that would hinder a quick exit.

I watched as Blaine and Meri got off the bus and walked toward their old double-wide mobile home. The orchard that surrounded the lane blocked the rest of my view. I figured that if I saw an unknown vehicle turn into their drive, I could speedily go and save them. *This is insane*, I thought. *I should just go and fetch Blaine and Meri and let Danny worry where they are when he gets home.* Instead, I heeded Lacey's request to not engage with Danny, and I waited there until I saw his truck arrive. My binoculars weren't powerful enough to see if Selena was with him.

It seemed to me the only way I could help Lacey would be through prayer. *Lord, please bring about the highest good and the best possible outcome for Lacey and her children.* Deep down, I felt that He heard my prayers and all would be okay once again.

chapter 4

Lacey loved large family gatherings. Over the years, Danny sometimes joined us but often feigned sickness and stayed home. That Christmas Eve, it surprised me when he arrived with Lacey and her children, especially since he was still seeing Selena.

Blaine and Meri usually exploded through my kitchen door in anticipation of opening presents on Christmas. That afternoon, they shuffled in behind Lacey, their eyes doleful, instead. Snuggling them into my arms for a hug, I watched as Danny bypassed me and trailed Lacey into the living room.

This was the first time I had seen him up close since I'd learned of the affair. I lengthened my embrace of my grandkids and tried to calm the bitterness I felt toward their stepfather. Blaine and Meri should be carefree at their tender ages, not subjected to the seediness of an affair.

The tension between Lacey and Danny was palpable as they sat side by side on the couch. It was as if there were a barrier between them that prohibited touching. My heart broke for Lacey. Christmas was her favorite holiday. She would plan months in advance to make sure her kids had what they wished for under the tree. She baked and decorated sugar cookies with them and always participated in the local sharing trees to provide gifts for those less fortunate. She donated to the food bank so families in need would have the fixings for Christmas dinner.

Even on non-holidays, Lacey was charitable. She took in friends who were down on their luck and provided them with a warm place to stay. She bought groceries for some of Danny's friends who struggled to feed their children and purchased diapers for their babies. Friends and family were important to her.

The pictures I took of Lacey, Danny, Blaine, and Meri in front of the Christmas tree that evening reflected a grim portrait of a family in turmoil. *Please, Lord, wrap Your protective arms around Lacey and my grandkids*, I pleaded silently. *Protect Blaine and Meri's fledgling minds from absorbing what is happening at home. Please keep their emotional scars minimal.*

⚙

Typically, I dedicate the week after Christmas to completing the restaurant's year-end reports, preparing W-2s, and tallying totals for tax returns. That year, however, I found myself unable to concentrate on forms or calculations. I'd sit down at my desk with good intentions—a detailed list of items to accomplish—but my mind forever veered to Lacey and her children.

So I fine-tuned my prayer ritual instead. I practiced inhaling deeply, and on the exhale, I relaxed my shoulders, tilted my chin up, closed my eyes, and furled my chest heavenward like a kite catching an air current. Focusing on my requests—protection for my grandchildren and the highest good in my family's lives—I imagined how it would feel when God granted it. I pictured my grandkids safe and Lacey happy. I trusted that my prayers would be blessed according to His plan. My God was good. My God was worthy of my trust and my love. My God protected my family. He always had. I assumed He always would.

Calls from Lacey became daily, then twice a day, three times, and I began to dread seeing my own daughter's name in the caller ID box of my phone. A tenseness invaded my neck muscles each time the phone rang, and I'd be tempted to not answer it. I'd feel like a horrible mother, not relishing that she wanted to share what was going on in her life. But each phone call was the same theme, over and over. Danny would tell Lacey he loved her and wanted to stay with her and the kids, and then he would stay out late to be with Selena. My vexation at what he was doing to Lacey kept building.

Then, one day, Lacey called with the news that Selena was pregnant. There was a chance it was Danny's child. Selena's former boyfriend—then in jail—believed it was his.

"Lacey, you need to kick his ass out," I said. "For heaven's sake, can't you see the damage he's doing to you and the kids?"

"But Mom, I love him."

"Oh, sweetie, I'm sure you think you do. But he's cheating on you! He needs to make a choice."

"I know, Mom. It's just . . . complicated."

A few weeks later, Lacey stopped by my house on her way to work.

I studied her as she sat on the raised bar stool, her hands lying limp in her lap. "What's up?" I asked. "Are you okay, sweetie?"

"Selena is missing, Mom."

"What do you mean, *missing*?"

"No one has seen or heard from her."

"Maybe she's just passed out somewhere. Did you tell Danny he needed to make a decision, either her or you?"

"Yeah. He stayed home last night, for the first time in ages." She sighed. "I think it was purely out of guilt, though. He slept on the couch."

"Maybe she saw his truck at home and got upset. Maybe she's moved on to someone else?"

"I suppose that could explain it," Lacey said, already getting up to leave. "I'll stop in at the restaurant later and let you know."

I was visiting with my staff and touching base with my kitchen to be sure the specialty items for upcoming banquets were ordered when the phone rang.

Seconds later, my floor manager motioned me over. She covered the mouthpiece with her hand, and asked, "Hey Bonnie, did you hear of a drug bust that went bad last night?"

"Who wants to know?" I asked, thinking how odd it was to receive a phone call asking for that type of information.

"They say they are from a Spokane news outlet," she answered.

"Nope, haven't heard of anything,"

Grabbing the glass coffee pot from its hot plate, I proceeded on my usual round of visiting customers and refilling their cups. I take pleasure in walking through the dining room and discovering where our patrons are from and why they have stopped at our restaurant. It is usually the highlight of my workday.

At the first table, an older couple was waiting for their friends and wanted to chat to pass the time. Another table showed me pictures of their new grandson and proclaimed how much they liked the newest server I had hired. At the last table, two longtime customers were just finishing their meal as I topped off their coffee.

"Say," I said, "we received a strange call about a drug bust last night. Have you heard anything?"

They both shook their heads. Then the wife said, "There was a female body found on a remote road. Maybe that has a connection."

"Maybe," I said as I cleared their plates.

Lacey called me later while I was in my office counting tills. She had talked to Danny. Selena's family had been asked to identify the body.

Reflecting on that moment, I realize it was never on my radar to connect Lacey with the "body found." Lacey was married to Danny. Danny's girlfriend was dead. Drugs were involved. I never once thought that Lacey would be blamed for Selena's death.

chapter 5

OROVILLE WOMAN'S DEATH BEING
INVESTIGATED AS A HOMICIDE
Selena Clark, 25, of Oroville, WA, was found dead at
the end of a driveway in the Pine Creek area on Sunday,
March 1, at 12:20 p.m.

Ron and I were at home reading the local paper when Lacey called and asked us to come out to her house. We arrived to find her and Danny in the living room with a single lamp casting a dim glow. Blaine and Meri were at a friend's house.

Lacey attempted a smile of welcome as she slouched in an overstuffed chair. Ron and I took a seat on the well-worn sofa next to Duke, their doe-eyed brown-and-white pit bull; his head lifted when I nudged him, but his massive body stayed glued in place. I massaged his soft fur. Danny tromped from the living room to the kitchen, then back to stand next to Lacey. I sent her a questioning look. Danny plopped down on the arm of the chair, and puffs of dust and dog hair floated upward.

Lacey started to tell us about events that had led up to the body being found. "I rented a van from work and gave it to Carly to use last Thursday and Friday."

"Is this the Carly you and Danny went to school with?" I asked.

"Yes," Lacey tucked a fleece blanket around her legs. "Carly was supposed to have the van back Saturday morning."

I listened but wondered what this had to do with us being there.

Lacey inhaled deeply, and on the exhale said, "I think Carly used the van to kill Selena."

My eyebrows shot up. "What? I don't understand."

Danny vaulted up and away from Lacey, then looped back and yelled, "What the fuck are you saying, Lacey?"

Now I understood why Lacey wanted us there. We were the cushion she needed as she explained the rental van to Danny.

Lacey glared at him, then turned toward Ron and me. "Carly has some crazy deep drug connections, and she thought Selena was going to narc on her. I think Carly took Selena in the van and had a couple of thugs beat her up." Lacey paused. "Since my name is on the rental van, fingers could point to me."

As Lacey's words registered, I thought, *With all of her sharing lately, how did she omit this gigantic detail? Crazy deep drug connections?*

"When Carly returned the van to me, she came this close," Lacey said, demonstrating by putting her hand three inches from her nose. "She looked me hard in the eye and said, 'You know what happens to people who talk." Lacey shuddered. "I'm afraid Carly will hurt the kids and me."

Danny paced to the kitchen and over to the front door. Clutching the doorknob, he turned and bellowed, "What the fuck have you done, Lacey? You know Carly has multiple personalities. What the fuck were you thinking?"

"I don't know, Danny," Lacey yelled back at him. "Carly asked for the van, and since she's your friend, I thought if I did something for her, you would be nicer to me."

My heart hurt for my daughter as I heard her desolation.

Danny yanked the door open and stormed out. Lacey collapsed into her chair. Ron positioned himself between Lacey and the door.

I took a calming breath to remove the daggers I'd felt when Danny threw the F-bombs. When I hear that word, I feel like my shoulder blades are being electrocuted. It makes me recoil, especially when it is yelled as violently as Danny had done.

"What do we need to do, Lacey?" I asked.

"I don't know, Mom. I just don't feel safe here."

Their rutted, one-lane road dead-ended at their house allowing no escape if Carly sought to hurt them.

"You could stay with us for a while," I offered. "It will be tight, but you would be safer there." Our house is in the center of our forty acres. The quarter-mile-long driveway exposes anyone who might approach.

Lacey went outside to find Danny, and I could hear his exasperation as they discussed it on the weather-beaten front porch.

"Fuck it, Lacey. I don't know what to do." His footsteps clomped back and forth. "Maybe that would be best, at least for the kids."

In our small town, we know the local police—their first name, where they live, who their kids are, and what they drive when they are off duty. They are an essential part of the community, and they have our respect. Ron and I had been raised to trust the law, and we had taught our two daughters the same values, so when Lacey chose to call the lead investigator in the case, it seemed the right thing to do. He said he would come to our house later that day.

We had kept the kids home for two days, but since the investigator was coming, I drove them to school. Dropping them as close to the front entrance as possible, I watched as Blaine gently nudged Meri with his backpack and then ran ahead of her. Meri ran to catch up with him, and my heart tugged as I saw how happy they looked to be released from the confines of my house and back to their regular routine. I watched as they entered the safety of the school; then I pulled into a parking space and surveyed the school surroundings until the bell rang. I was mindful of cars behind me, parked in strange places, and idling in the lot like I was. Could I keep my grandkids safe? What if something happened to them while they were in my care? I imagined horrible scenarios of them being kidnapped and held hostage. Would the kidnapper trick the secretary in the school office by saying there was an emergency at home and he had been sent to pick the kids up? Would a large black sedan with tinted windows zoom through the parking lot, stop quickly beside them, and whisk them away?

The bell rang, and students who had arrived late rushed to enter the school.

As I drove home, I sent up prayers: *Lord, please keep my family safe.* My eyes glanced upward, seeking connection with Him, and then settled to the task of driving. It was distracted prayer—different from being able to close my eyes, go keenly inward, and feel God's love surrounding me. When I can concentrate fully on prayer, I feel a blanket of protection flow from my head and wrap around my shoulders. This time, I didn't feel the calm.

Arriving home, I straightened up our master bedroom, sprayed vanilla-scented air freshener, and set up two padded folding chairs. Lacey would talk to the police in there.

The lead investigator was Matt Hoover. Ron and I had known him since he married the ex-wife of one of our cooks many years ago. Matt was tall and lean, with a receding hairline and trimmed gray mustache. A few years back, Ron's dad, a county commissioner at the time, had been instrumental in appointing him as interim sheriff. Matt had run for election that fall and lost; upon his defeat, he'd returned to being undersheriff.

He arrived with Deputy Paul Baker, a likable young man who seemed to know Danny. Danny's mom also joined us. She was the bar manager at our larger restaurant.

Lacey went with Matt and the deputy into the master bedroom and closed the door. I pictured her sitting cross-legged in the middle of our bed, although I never asked her later whether that was how she actually positioned herself while speaking to the officers.

In the living room, the rest of us didn't even attempt small talk. Danny paced the floor and went outside to smoke. His mom followed him. When they returned, the aroma of tobacco drifted in behind them.

At first, Danny sat rigid on the couch. Then he dropped his head, raked his fingers through his hair, and buried his face in his hands. His rattled gestures increased with the amount of time Lacey talked with the deputies. Every once in a while, he went outside. Whenever he came back in, the lingering smell of cigarette smoke was magnified.

Time seemed to drag. I sat upright in my recliner with an outward look of calm, but my right foot betrayed me. It's a telltale sign my family knows well. The more agitated I get, the faster my foot jigs. Danny's endless activity vexed me, and my foot vibrated like a broken weathervane shimmying in a storm.

When Lacey and the deputies finally emerged, Matt remained in the living room while the other deputy and Danny went outside. I wanted to ask Lacey how it had gone. Would Matt be able to protect her? Did she feel safer now that she had told them about the threat to her life? It didn't seem like the appropriate time to ask those questions, so I stayed mute. Matt (I have a hard time calling him Deputy Hoover) was a known and trusted entity. I believed he would keep Lacey from harm.

Ron asked, "Matt, do we need a lawyer for Lacey?"

Matt shook his head. "She's not a suspect, Ron."

Danny, Deputy Baker, and Matt proceeded to the master bedroom for Danny's statement. I hadn't realized Danny was going to give a statement too. It made more sense now why his mom was there.

Lacey sat on the couch nearest the bedroom, attempting to hear Danny and the investigators. Danny's mom slid over next to her. Lacey's concentration on eavesdropping precluded any conversation we might have had. My foot continued its gyrations.

Thirty minutes later, Danny joined his mom and Lacey on the couch while both officers stepped outside to talk privately. Danny slipped his arm around Lacey, and they conversed in whispered tones.

When Matt returned, he asked, "Lacey, could you and Danny leave town for a few days, maybe a week, while we continue our investigation?"

Lacey looked at Ron and me and asked, "You okay with watching the kids that long?"

"Yeah, we could do that," I answered for both of us. "Where would you go?"

"Doesn't matter where," Matt interjected, "just out of town. Danny, I don't want you to contact any of your usual people."

The plan was set in motion. Blaine and Meri would stay with us.

The other deputy looked at Danny and said in a concerned voice, "Danny, this would be a good time to get off the meth."

I glanced at Lacey. She gave me a slight head nod, confirming Deputy Baker's statement. Scrutinizing Danny's face, I noticed that his eyes were deep-set and hollow, and he had scabbed-over bumps on his face that made it look like he had cut himself shaving. His body was gaunt. I knew he smoked pot, but meth? I visualized the Health Department brochure, "Meth and Its Destruction," that I had read a week earlier while waiting for a food-handlers' class to begin. The glossy pictures on the front flap had shown disheveled meth users with rotten teeth, sunken eyes, and faces pockmarked with open sores. Before this moment, when I had looked at Danny, all I'd seen was Lacey's husband.

✶—✶—✶—✶—✦

I continued to drive Blaine and Meri to and from school for the next week, diligently waiting outside until I knew they were safe inside. In the afternoons, I arrived fifteen minutes before release time, careful to park near the front door. Each day, once they emerged from the school and were safely seated inside my SUV, I sent up acknowledgment: *Thank You, Lord, for their safety today.* I'd take them for ice cream, and we'd kick a soccer ball around or bake cookies after we got home. In the evenings, I helped them with homework. After dinner, we'd play UNO or a game of Sorry.

When Danny and Lacey returned from their week of hiding, they relocated back to their own house. My mind whirled. *Is it safe? Has the threat passed? Is Danny off the meth?*

chapter 6

CARLY REEVES ARRESTED IN MURDER OF PREGNANT WOMAN

Detectives arrested a 29-year-old woman in the murder of a pregnant Oroville woman and are searching for a second suspect.

A second person was arrested—the "taxman" (this, I learned, was slang for the enforcer of payment in the drug world). Two people were now behind bars. Their mug shots on the front page of the local weekly newspaper portrayed unkempt hair and piercing eyes.

The criminals responsible for the upheaval in our lives were behind bars. *Thank You, Lord, for ending this nightmare. Thank You for protecting my family.*

When I arrived home from work a few days later, there was an unmarked navy blue squad car sitting next to Lacey's car. Ron was out in his woodshop. Matt had arrived with a different deputy than before and had asked Ron to call Lacey to come and talk with them again.

Ron told me he had again asked Matt if we needed a lawyer.

"We have no intention of arresting her," Matt said. "We just want some clarification on her first statement."

My mama-bear instinct engaged as I walked to the house and entered my kitchen. Matt, the new deputy, and Lacey were sitting in the living room. Conversation stopped when they saw me. I don't remember if I said anything, but it was evident by their silence that they didn't want me there. I walked back out to the shop and summoned strength from God, tilting my face toward heaven. *Lord, please guide me. Show me what I need to do.*

Ron was at his workbench in the middle of the room. The circular blade on the table saw was running, and I watched as he deftly measured and cut lengths of two-by-fours. *Zingg.* The saw cutting through the wood was loud and shrill.

Ron had on the red, white, and blue cap that he had received for being a volunteer firefighter and ambulance driver in our hometown. Sawdust shavings sat on the hat's visor, and some had migrated to his salt-and-pepper beard.

My mind traveled back to the living room. *Why are they questioning Lacey again? What more can she tell them? Is Danny being implicated? They already arrested Carly and that other man; why are they still investigating?*

Matt stepped out the front door and walked in our direction. I alerted Ron, and he shut off the saw. Matt stopped midway between the house and shop, motioned for us to come his way, and then walked away before we could join him.

Ron brushed the sawdust off his jeans as we progressed toward the house. Married almost forty years, we've become accustomed to communicating by silent osmosis; we trust each other to be on the same page in any situation, without discussion. I've always felt incredibly blessed by that.

We joined Lacey in the living room while both deputies went outside to talk.

Lacey sat in Ron's oversized recliner, knees bent and feet tucked under her. I sat likewise, on the floor next to her. Ron remained standing.

The deputies returned, and Matt sat down on the brown suede ottoman with his long legs bent and his feet compressing the plush carpet. He rested his elbows on his knees, pressed his palms flat together, and touched his chin with the tips of his long fingers. The other deputy stood near the front door.

Matt spoke guardedly. "We are going to arrest Lacey."

Ron stepped toward him. "You said you weren't here to arrest her."

Matt's elbows remained on his knees, but his sitting posture stiffened. "We are arresting Lacey for her own protection," he said. "We waited until today, after the local paper went to print, to give you some time before it hits the news." As he spoke each sentence, his body rocked forward and backward. He was lulling us, and his mentioning her protection soothed us like it was meant to. He leaned in again. "You can bail her out tomorrow. We brought an unmarked car so we'd be less conspicuous, but it doesn't have the Plexiglas divider, so we'll have to put her in handcuffs."

My hands began to shake. The trembling climbed my arms until it reached my neck. I shuddered as if I'd been deluged by an ice storm. Ron put a protective hand on Lacey's shoulder. My body felt immovable. Tears rolled down my cheeks as I looked at my daughter and my husband. Matt walked to the door while the other deputy went to the squad car for the handcuffs.

Lacey rose slowly, and I watched as Ron encircled her with his strong arms. When I tried to stand up, I felt like a feeble old woman with wobbly legs. Ron reached out to steady me.

The late-afternoon sun glinted off the leaded-glass door as both deputies waited on the front porch to handcuff our daughter. She presented her hands to Matt. He secured the cuffs and led her down the three steps to the sidewalk. Ron and I watched as the second deputy draped her with a belly chain and attached leg shackles. I clutched Ron's bicep for balance and looked toward heaven with sinking disbelief. *Where are You, God?*

Lacey's restraints rattled as she was stowed in the front seat. Matt squished into the back between stacks of paperwork. They drove away swiftly, and the raised dust from their tires chased after them, just as I was tempted to do. The fine particles settled back to the earth before Ron and I went inside.

chapter 7

I was four months pregnant with Lacey when we moved to a small ranch just north of town. Ron's dad's restaurant was up for sale, so Ron went to work tending cattle.

The salary was $400 a month, a rent-free house, fresh eggs, and free beef. The house sat on a knoll. Branches from a Chinese elm tree drooped over the eaves of the second story. A chicken coop provided shelter for a dozen free-range hens. One of the chickens had gained access to the house through a broken bathroom window, and when we walked inside one day, we found several eggs on the black-and-white battleship linoleum, near the warmth of the hot water tank. Downy white pinfeathers and a few reddish-brown ones gave us a clue as to which chicken had claimed that area her own. My parents later told their friends that I had to shoo the chickens out to be able to move in.

I swept and scrubbed and sewed homemade curtains. Ron repaired the window and trimmed some of the large overhanging tree branches. In the fall of 1974, that work done, we moved into the ramshackle farmhouse.

While Ron worked on the ranch, I kept our wood stove stoked with the kindling he chopped and learned how to turn the chimney damper to the correct angle to hold the heat longer. I hand-stitched a small quilt for our unborn baby, attaching a starburst of pale Delft blue onto a soft yellow background. Quarter-size saffron-yellow circles were at the center of each design. I mastered the necessary skill of using a thimble as I stitched so I wouldn't poke my finger and stain the material. I nested and felt like a pioneer woman.

Ron drove the tractor and fed hay to the cattle herd. In the evenings during calving time, I rode with him in the pickup truck to check on the heifers. The bright spotlight reflected shiny orbs in their eyes as we searched for pregnant cows in trouble. Watching Ron use the calf-puller to extricate a baby calf stuck half in and half out of its mother's womb, I tried not to compare that problematic birth to our future one.

The months went by, and my belly grew. On the first day of fishing season, our daughter was born. Ron watched through the glass outside the delivery room because our rural hospital had yet to accept the progressive idea of fathers participating in the birth.

Lacey was the perfect baby. She ate heartily, slept soundly, and cooed at her loving family when she was awake. My mom arrived and stayed with us for a week to assist in my transition to motherhood. Her calm, nurturing ways were a godsend to Ron and me as we adjusted to our new role as parents.

We left the ranch a few months after Lacey was born. Our next house had a white picket fence that outlined the front yard. On the south side, tips of Kelly green corn stalks sprouted through the fertile soil of the newly tilled garden. Red and pink roses bloomed. The shade of a weeping white birch protected us on hot summer days. Our life was simple and good.

chapter 8

"Bail was set at a quarter of a million dollars," Ron said dragging out the *millllllion*. "That means we need to come up with ten percent of that to bail her out." He paused. "Where do we pull the funds from?"

My business brain considered our options. "Do we bail her out or do we save the bail money for her defense?"

"The lawyer said it could take up to two years in a case like this," Ron said. "He feels it would be advantageous for Lacey if it does take a long time."

"It hasn't even been twenty-four hours since her arrest, and now we are talking two years? How can it possibly take two years?" My voice spiraled with anger. "I don't understand how they could arrest her in the first place. She didn't do anything wrong. What if we don't have enough money after we bail her out to pay for two years of legal-fees?"

Ron's eyes filled as he shook his head side to side. "I can't leave her sitting in jail."

The following day we drove to the bank, withdrew $25,000 from our savings account, and purchased a cashier's check payable to the bail bonds office. As Ron drove, I positioned the check neatly on my lap and closed my eyes. *Dear Lord, please allow today to go smoothly.*

Across the street from the county jail, a sign reading "AAA Bail Bonds" in gold-faded lettering assured us we were in the right place. In smaller letters, underneath, were the words "Quick, Fair, and Confidential."

The weathered brown door creaked as we entered. A massive wooden desk, stained with water rings, commandeered most of the room. The bail bondsman pulled forms from the file drawer, then hesitated, removed a page, and set it on top of the cabinet.

"We won't need that form, Mr. and Mrs. Hirst," he explained as he placed the remaining pile of paperwork in front of us. "Normally you would need to sign a lien against your home for this amount of bail. You're business owners, so I'll forgo that."

My eyes closed and my palm rested on the pale green cashier's check. *Thank You, Lord.* I hadn't even considered that we would have to put our house on the line too. The bail bondsman receives 10 percent of the amount set for bail. No refunds. By posting bond, Ron and I were guaranteeing that Lacey wouldn't skip town. If she did, we would be responsible for the entire quarter million.

We signed multiple forms in triplicate, each with Lacey's name and case number printed boldly across the top. When the time came to pay the bond fee, I placed the pristine check on the worn desktop. The bail bondsman covered it with his long fingers and slid it to the edge of the desk. After glancing at the amount, he folded the check in half and then half again, and paper-clipped it to the top of Lacey's forms. He handed us a clearance paper to take to the jail and chucked her file onto his growing stack of papers.

From the bail bond office, we proceeded to the jail. The entrance, with its concrete and metal overhang, appeared to be taking us underground. Ron pulled the gray metal door open and waited for me to enter. I hesitated. He opened it wider, and we walked in together.

In the waiting room, two metal benches were bolted to the wall. A raised, glassed-in workstation safeguarded the visiting area. Ron placed the bail papers into an open vault drawer similar to those used at drive-through bank windows. It clanged closed, and a female voice came over the garbled intercom. "We will process this, and Lacey should be released soon."

The buzz of the intercom stopped. I could see the woman talking to someone else, but no sound escaped. *Are they discussing business or gossiping about us?* I felt diminished, like someone needing pity. *Can they still hear us?*

Ron and I sat solemnly on the cold metal bench. After a few minutes' wait, a loud buzzer sounded on a door next to us. Lacey walked through as it opened, wearing the clothes she had been arrested in. Her face reflected relief and gratitude as Ron and I ushered her to the exit.

The lawyer's office was the next stop. Parking our car on Main Street, I felt conspicuous, like we were announcing to everyone that we needed a criminal lawyer. We'd never been involved with the justice system before, so we hadn't known who to turn to when Lacey was arrested. The attorney we used for our wills had recommended Jack Haney, a lawyer who had recently moved to town.

Haney's secretary escorted Ron, Lacey, and me down a narrow hallway and stopped in front of an old-time walk-in safe. It even had the circular turnstile wheel on the outside. The thick metal door stood open. Inside, Haney sat at a large desk wedged into the safe's interior. His tailored dark gray suit complemented his silver hair. He stood as we entered, removed his black-rimmed reading glasses, and shook our hands across the desktop. My first impression was good. Neat in appearance. Respectful demeanor.

He presented paperwork for Ron and me to sign that stated we were responsible for his fees—which included an exorbitant retainer—but that we would not be privy to the conversations or information exchanged between Lacey and him. The paperwork was clearly a standard form; our names were inserted into blank white spaces. Was this a regular occurrence, parents signing away their right to know what they were paying for? In the tight space that was his office, with its thick insulated walls, I felt stifled yet hopeful. We had been thrown into an unknown realm of lawyers, bail bonds, legal terms, and court dates. I felt like we were drowning. I hoped Haney would be our lifeline.

⁎ ⁎ ⁎ ⁎ ⁎

There was no conversation in the car on the way home. Ron was at the wheel, I was in the passenger seat, and Lacey sat in the back like a reprimanded teenager being driven home by her parents. Country music played softly on the radio. My feelings of gratitude that she was safe—*Thank You, Lord*—made tears well in my eyes. Any words I tried to form were strangled by the deep sorrow I felt for my daughter. I wanted to ask if she had been treated okay. Had the handcuffs hurt her wrists? Did she like the attorney we had hired? Was she hungry? I adjusted the visor so she couldn't see my tears.

chapter 9

Lacey's mug shot filled the TV screen on the morning news show. The camera flash had turned her pupils red, and she looked haunted in the jail-issued jumpsuit with her messy hair and chapped lips. I fumbled with the remote and hit the pause button. Staring back at me, Lacey's face was ashen. Her eyes appeared puffy, like she had been crying. My heart clutched seeing the fear and demoralization that the camera had captured. Had the jail taken only one picture of her, or many? Had they picked the one where she looked the most disturbed?

I pushed the play button, seeking to remove the frozen, pain-filled picture from my vision. The reporter read his script: "Wife arrested for hiring a hit man to murder her husband's pregnant girlfriend." Shivers rained through my body. The reporter sounded so matter-of-fact. He may as well have said, *Of course she's guilty, she's been arrested. Why wouldn't she want her husband's girlfriend gone?*

He moved on to the next story.

So much for waiting for the weekly paper before everyone found out. I felt like thunderbolts had struck my body. Nausea and claustrophobia ambushed me as if I were caged inside a disproportionately tiny box. *Lord, please give me strength.*

When I called my dad in Phoenix, he greeted me with his usual, "Hi Bonnie, I'm glad you called." He had read the caller ID and was expecting our weekly chat.

"Hey, Dad," I said. "How's your week going?"

"Good . . . what's wrong, Bonnie? Your voice sounds off."

"I think maybe you should sit down, Dad."

I could imagine his happiness deflating over the long-distance line. "I'm sitting. Is this an April Fool's joke or something?"

"Oh, Dad, I wish it were." I pictured him sitting in his La-Z-Boy recliner, looking out at the white-rocked patio area, landscaped with barrel cactus and agave plants. "Lacey was arrested, Dad." I tried to soften the blow for him, "Long story short: Danny cheated on her. The girlfriend is dead. Fingers are pointing at Lacey." I quickly added, "I'm sure it will all work itself out."

"What was the charge?" he asked. He had been a police officer before I was born. He'd once shown me photos of his first crime scene, a homicide. The black-and-white picture had shown a man lying in a pool of dark liquid at the bottom of a concrete stairwell.

"I'm not sure," I said. "We go to court next week for that."

There was a long pause. I heard him blow his nose. I pictured him folding his white handkerchief and putting it back into his pants pocket.

"It'll be okay, Dad, I just wanted you to know."

Years later, he told me he wept for three days.

chapter 10

My ordered world disintegrated, and I melted into myself like plastic torched with flame. In my mind, I blamed Danny, the drugs, the detectives, and Carly. There was no way Lacey had done this. Then my distraught brain pointed the blame toward me. Why had I not seen how dire her situation was? We should have lawyered up and prevented her from giving statements. I should have been able to put a stop to this. *Dear Lord, please guide me. Give me the strength to shoulder this burden. Please watch over my family and help this nightmare turn into a blessing.*

It had been several days since Lacey's arrest. I needed to go to the restaurant and prepare deposits. I hadn't slept well and had risen early.

Driving the twenty-minute route, I was treated to golden sunbeams glistening off the rising mist of the river. Such a peaceful scene. God's presence in nature always soothes me, and I felt He was sending me a message: *"Be calm, Bonnie."*

Thank You, Lord, for the natural beauty that surrounds me. Thank You for the peace I find in nature. Help me to remember and maintain this pastoral feeling today.

Entering the bustling kitchen of the restaurant, I saw my head cook busy on the grill. He looked up and nodded, but didn't greet me with his usual, "Good morning, Bonnie." He returned to tending the food on the flat-top. The prep cook was dicing onions and green peppers for omelet mix. She acknowledged me with a sad and knowing look. By their nonverbal communication, I knew they had heard about Lacey and were waiting for me to initiate the conversation.

I couldn't greet them with my standard, "Hey, how's it going today?" Instead, I walked silently through the kitchen and down the waitress hallway. My opening server was stacking dirty plates on the bus cart. The mid-shift girl was entering new food orders into the computer. They both glanced my way as I poured myself a cup of coffee, but neither one said anything as I went into my office.

Closing the door, I leaned against it and sipped my steaming brew. So this was how it was going to be—no one knowing what to say. Me included.

Counting the first day's receipts, I was unable to balance sales against cash. Re-counting, I double-checked gift cards sold, gift cards redeemed, and cash payouts, but I was still short twenty-one dollars. What were a few dollars in the backwash of the last few days? With four other tills to count, my fingers felt disjointed on the adding machine, and I failed to balance each day's debits with credits.

I filled out deposit slips, bundled the money for each day into a bank bag, and opened the office door. The smell of frying bacon and freshly cooked pancakes with warm maple syrup wafted to my nostrils. At this point in my day, I would usually walk to the cook line and find two slices of crisp bacon waiting for me. I tuned in to the sound of satisfied patrons in conversation and heard the ding of the front door signaling the arrival of additional customers.

I ducked out the exit-only door closest to my office without talking to anyone.

Tears flowed down my face as I got in my car. God's communiqué that morning, reminding me to remain calm, was not working. My nerves were jagged and raw like they had been scraped over the sharp edges of a vegetable grater. Covering my face with my hands, I sobbed uncontrollably. I cried for my daughter, my grandkids, my husband, and myself. I cried for my tired brain that continued to spin with unanswered questions. I hated that I had to attend to business when all I wanted was to be at home. I wanted to close every blind in the house, climb into bed, and hide under the covers, forever. Lacey's situation was not in my scope of problem-solving. I felt helpless and overwhelmed.

I composed myself enough to drive downtown to the bank. Upon arriving there, I was thankful for the ability to put the deposits into the night drop and not have to stand in line. This larger town afforded me more anonymity than our hometown, but what I would have given for an invisible woman costume, to be able to complete my responsibilities without anyone seeing me, in either town.

The crying jag had helped remove some of my *poor me* emotions, but as I drove home, my anger surfaced. Pounding the steering wheel with the heel of my hand, I screamed out loud. "Why didn't Danny keep his zipper shut? Damn it! Lacey should have left him like I told her to. It's like I'm waiting for the next frigging shoe to drop so I can pick up those pieces too. Shit! Will everything Ron and I have spent a lifetime working for go down the drain? Our good name, our reputation, and possibly our income? Fuuuck!"

chapter 11

TWO MORE ACCUSED

More grisly details surfaced last week with the arrest of two additional suspects in the beating and stabbing death of a 25-year-old woman. Lacey Hirst-Pavek is accused of offering $500 for the killing and renting a car that detectives said was used in the attack. She was released last week from the county jail on $250,000 bail and is charged with conspiracy to commit first-degree murder and conspiracy to commit first-degree manslaughter. Mark Peterson was also arrested for allegedly supplying the murder weapon.

A week after Lacey's arrest, we attended her arraignment. This, we learned, was where she would plead not guilty to the charges. Lacey, Ron, and I listened as Haney—outside the courtroom—explained what we could expect from Judge Cone during the proceedings. Before Cone became a judge, he had practiced law in our hometown and frequented our first restaurant. We weren't friends with him, but he knew who we were.

The court docket was full. Haney explained that since Lacey had a private attorney, her case would go before those with appointed lawyers. We followed him through the metal detector and entered to find the wooden benches three-quarters full. Lacey whispered to Ron and me that Selena's family and friends filled the two back rows. They shot vile, venomous looks toward Lacey. I hadn't considered that her family might be there. Haney had said it would be a simple form-filing morning.

We selected seats as far away from Selena's family as possible. Ron and I sheltered Lacey between us as we waited for the judge to enter and court to start. Haney had been wrong. There would be nothing simple about this.

Two other cases went before us, but I was too distraught about Selena's family's presence to even grasp what they were about. When Lacey's name was called, my pulse surged; its cadence in my carotid arteries reverberated throughout my body as if I had taken a deep-water dive, and the outside pressure was about to burst my blood vessels. As Lacey joined Haney at the large table, I took a deep breath and willed myself to calm down. *Dear Lord, be with us.* I noticed a slight touch of improvement.

There was loud whispering behind us from Selena's family. In the front row, two newspaper reporters opened their notebooks, pens poised and ready. I hadn't noticed them writing anything down before Lacey's case was called.

The reading of the documents took about fifteen minutes. The prosecutor had requested that Lacey and Danny be separated—no contact, since Danny could be a witness in the other three suspects' trials, and the prosecutor thought Lacey could sway his testimony. Rather contradictory, I thought, since the investigators had already sent them off together for a week before Lacey's arrest. Did the judge not know that? Was this normal, to keep spouses apart? Haney had told us that husbands and wives couldn't testify against each other, so this request was a surprise.

Haney suggested to the judge that the no-contact order would create difficulties with Lacey's minor children and their school activities and living arrangements. Judge Cone looked pointedly to Ron and me and asked if we would be willing to facilitate any information exchange regarding the children and transfer them between parents when needed. I nodded. Ron said, "Yes, Your Honor." Judge Cone granted the no-contact order and attached it to Lacey's other bail requirements, which were:

- May not leave the county
- Needs to check in with bail bondsman M-W-F
- No contact with State's witnesses
- May not possess firearms or dangerous weapons
- May not drink intoxicating liquor or be where alcohol is sold by the drink
- May not possess controlled substances except as prescribed by a physician
- May not violate any laws

I had naively fixated on one word that had been printed in the newspaper: "conspiracy." To me, it sounded innocuous. Neither murder nor manslaughter had registered in my overwrought brain. I didn't understand until after Lacey's trial that charging her with conspiracy was the simplest way for the prosecution to pull her into their web.

Later, when I Googled *conspiracy*, I found that under most states' conspiracy laws, each conspirator can be held legally responsible for any crimes committed by other conspirators. However, each conspirator does not decide the scope of the conspiracy for him or herself. Instead, even one co-conspirator can broaden the scope of the conspiracy. In other words, a conspirator can easily be held responsible for crimes that he or she did not plan to commit or even anticipate.

The court clerk announced the next case. Haney and Lacey stood and motioned us to leave with them. Passing back through the metal detector, we followed Haney as he moved farther away from the exit. We were still in a public area but not in the direct path of Selena's family as they were leaving. Two from their group veered off and strutted menacingly past us as if to say, "You'd better watch your back, Lacey. You could end up dead too."

RELATIVES REACT TO CHARGINGS

Angry relatives of a slain woman crowded into a small courtroom to show their displeasure with those charged.

After the arraignment, and the order for Danny and Lacey to be separated, Ron set up our travel trailer near his shop as Lacey's new home. Blaine and Meri were with Danny during the week and with Lacey on the weekends. It saddened me, her being apart from them, but she wanted her children to be in their own beds on school nights—to disrupt their lives as little as possible.

chapter 12

AFFAIR MAY HAVE TRIGGERED
ICE PICK SLAYING
An Oroville woman who was beaten and stabbed to
death with an ice pick was the apparent victim of a
murder-for-hire plot. Police say it appears that Lacey
Hirst-Pavek's husband was having an affair with
Selena Clark, who was pregnant. When Hirst-Pavek
found out, she began making comments that she wanted
Clark dead and talked with others about having Clark
beaten up.

Townsfolk had their own take on our situation. I saw it on the faces of people I met when I was in town: repelled looks from some; averted eyes from others. At the grocery store, acquaintances would veer into the next aisle when they saw me. Those who did approach had experienced challenging times in their own lives. They offered hugs or said quietly in my ear, "I'm thinking about you" or "You are in my prayers." Their empathy tugged at my heart and strangled my voice. I pulled crumpled tissues from my pockets to dab at my eyes.

Several "Thinking about You" notes arrived in the mail, addressed to Ron and me, from old friends who inscribed thoughtful words in beautiful cards. At the time, I didn't grasp the magnitude of graciousness those short notes represented. I was more concerned with the conceptual devastation of my own world. I stashed the growing stack of cards into a cubbyhole in my desk.

Lacey was functioning as well as she could. Her kids were playing in a soccer tournament, and she and I took our lawn chairs like we did every year and watched from the sidelines. Instead of standard greetings from other parents, we received sharp glares and avoidance. We positioned ourselves away from the other spectators, but not far enough away for one of them. Tracy Felton, soccer mom extraordinaire, picked up her chair, cooler, and umbrella and moved farther away from us, protesting loudly like she was leading a charge, "How dare you even show your face in public, Lacey."

I wanted to come to Lacey's defense. I wanted to tell Tracy Felton to just wait until she was wrongly accused of something she didn't do, to wait until her life fell apart, and then see how it feels when people are spiteful. I wanted to tell her life isn't all about the perfect snacks, the perfect outfit, the latest hairdo. I wanted to scream in her face and make a huge scene. Instead, I watched Lacey's reaction.

Lacey held her head up and pretended not to hear Tracy's comment, or the whispering; she also pretended not to see the pointed fingers or turned heads. She cheered when her kids made good plays and when the team scored a goal. She showed grit. I took note of those who shunned her. I know it's not godly of me, but I told myself they'd better not seek employment at my restaurants in the future. This mother would never forget who they were.

I aspired to be by Lacey's side when she needed to be in public, to be there to protect her and cushion her from the accusing stares and hate she faced daily. The middle finger was often projected savagely at her in public. She told me it wasn't as pronounced when I was there. I could only imagine how bad it was when she was by herself.

When Lacey and I attended a school band concert to watch her son play the drums, there seemed to be an undertow of movement as people stepped aside. It appeared that the prescribed perimeter around us was about four feet; that, apparently, was far enough removed to make it clear they weren't aligned with us. One brave soul, the band director, came toward us with a smile. She hugged Lacey in front of everyone and whispered in her ear, "I'm praying for you." I was bowled over with gratitude. My eyes filled, and my face contorted grotesquely as I tried not to cry.

A web page had been created to offer Selena's family condolences and allow her friends to share their grief. Lacey followed it. The first few weeks, the posts were positive support and remembrances of Selena in her days before drugs. After the soccer tournament, however, the conversation thread degenerated into negative comments about Lacey:

> *How can Lacey be attending a public event for kids? She murdered Selena and her unborn baby, she shouldn't be allowed to be near other children. They should take her kids away from her for their personal safety. They shouldn't have allowed her out on bail.*

Lacey read the posts obsessively. I told her not to, but I also understood her need. It's like watching someone do a high-wire act without a net. You are scared to watch, and you hope the artist doesn't fall, but if he does, you will watch it—the falling. You might turn your head at the point of impact; or you might not.

Lacey was falling. I was falling. I also perused the web page and was pulled into the loathsome remarks. They would churn in my psyche all day.

What is Ron and Bonnie's last name? Are they Lacey's parents? How many children do these beasts Lacey and Danny have? I tell you, this just gets worse by the minute. How can bail only be $25,000? I tell you murder is cheap in Okanogan County . . . This is so messed up.

Boycotting her family's businesses seems like the only way to hurt Lacey's defense currently. They need the business to make money in order to pay for her fancy lawyer, but I bet most of the patrons don't even realize who they are giving their hard-earned money to. Does anyone know the names of everything her family owns? I can make some online posts and possibly take out an ad in one of the big newspapers in either Seattle or Spokane to make sure that those unaware of the situation don't accidentally stop at one of the places and hand their money over to murderers, but could someone in town post fliers or something?

Some people were brave enough to use their real names. Others posted behind fictitious labels like In the Know, Curious, What the Hell, and Dancing with the Devil. One even boasted of sending the story to Nancy Grace and Geraldo Rivera. I anguished over the day when national reporters would show up on my doorstep. I rationalized my need to read the comments, convincing myself it was imperative to know when and where to be alert. From which angle would the next threat come?

I was at our larger restaurant one morning when a tall, thin man asked to see the owner. When anyone comes in and doesn't know my name, I assume they are trying to sell something on a cold call.

I approached the entryway, where my staff had asked him to wait. His back was to the sun shining through the windows, and I was unable to see his face. I reached my hand out to shake his like I would do with any salesman, but his hands remained in his pockets. My eyes then took in his dirty, ripped jeans, and I knew he wasn't looking to sell me anything.

Shifting our positions so my back was to the windows and closer to the exit doors, I could see his sunken face, rotted teeth, and matted hair. His breath stank like an old ashtray as he towered over me.

"Are you that bitch Lacey's mom?" His voice echoed loudly in the entryway. One of my servers came to see what was happening. I jerked my head toward the kitchen, as in, *Go get one of the cooks to help me.* She disappeared quickly.

"I am," I responded as I continued to move slowly toward the exit door. He followed, keeping an equitable distance between us; at least he wasn't in attack mode. I saw my husky morning cook come out of the kitchen and follow, unobserved, behind the tall man.

"Let's step outside and talk," I said as I reached the door. I opened it and stepped out to the concrete walkway. When we were both outside, I asked him, "What can I do for you?"

My cook observed us from the entryway.

Slurring his words, he said, "Selena was my friend, and I miss her, and your daughter killed her, and I'm sad." His narrow shoulders drooped, his head tilted down, and he wiped his runny nose on his tattered sleeve. He began to sob.

"I'm sorry for your loss," I said. I wanted to put my hand on his shoulder to console him, but I worried he might get loud or angry again now that he had shared his sadness. "Do you have a car, or can I call you a cab?" I asked, wanting him off the premises as soon as possible.

"No, I walked from over there," he said, pointing to a new building a few blocks away.

"Okay," I said. "Why don't you walk back over there now?" I led him to the edge of the sidewalk, grateful that my cook was following behind. When the tall man stepped out on his own, I said, "I don't want you to come back to my restaurant again." He didn't respond as he walked away.

My body shivered with relief as I turned and entered the building with my bodyguard.

That confrontation could have gone so differently. *Thank You, Lord, for my protection today. Thank You for helping me defuse the situation.*

Lacey's arrest and the escalating headlines had now put me at risk. After that incident, I searched for ways to minimize my exposure. When I walked through my dining room, instead of stopping to visit each table like I used to, I'd survey the diners, pick out longtime customers who had kept coming in after Lacey's arrest, and talk only to them. Even though I prayed and believed God was with me, I was fretful. It wasn't long before I quit approaching any customers. I secluded myself in my office, available only when my problem-solving was absolutely necessary to keep the daily operations going.

chapter 13

My friend Nanc (pronounced Nance) called and left a message on the answering machine: "When you feel ready to talk or cry, just give me a call."

It took me a couple of days to phone her back. I thought I was composed enough to share details about Lacey, but when she answered with, "Bonnie, how are you?" all the fear and trying to be strong gushed into deep, gasping sobs.

I'm . . . sorry . . . Nanc," I managed to say, still crying. "I didn't call to blubber like an idiot." Sniffing my dripping nose, I pulled out a tissue and blew loudly.

"Take your time, Bonnie. I'm not going anywhere."

Instead of talking about the arrest, I told her about the arraignment and the terror I had felt being surrounded by hostile onlookers.

Al and Nanc live a hundred miles from us but have been close friends for many years. We met them while maintaining Forest Service trails in the mountains. Nanc is one of those friends who can go several months without talking to me, then call and pick up our last conversation like it was yesterday.

"Al and I will be there in court with you the next time," she told me. "You just let us know when and where."

I knew without a doubt they would both be there if I asked. Therein lay the problem. I was comfortable asking God for help, but to ask a friend or family member? That would mean I didn't have the answers. That I couldn't solve the problem. That I wasn't able to cope.

part 2

chapter 14

I sought solitude and peace on the lake next to our cabin. I slipped into the teal hull of my kayak, and I became one with the water. *Thank You, God, for this alone time.*

Gliding along the shoreline of the narrow lake, I watched as a mallard swam with her ducklings. Five of them played follow the leader up and over logs, their fuzzy bodies bobbing in sync on the lake's shimmering surface. Mama duck tracked behind the last baby as it scouted—in the opposite direction—a feather floating on the water. That's when she saw me. Quacking the alarm, and with outstretched wings, she hectically pushed the lagging baby forward. Her haste created a froth and a trail of bubbles. I back-paddled my kayak to give her more space. Squawking to her little ones, she maneuvered them all into the camouflage of the reeds. Their high-pitched cheeps quieted as they huddled down in the willowed grasses. I coveted the mama duck's ability to guide her brood to safety.

Paddling farther, I spotted a turtle with its outstretched neck basking in the sun on a half-submerged log. The blue sky was painted with wispy white clouds that looked like strokes from an artist's brush. Dragonflies darted over my kayak and landed on the front bow as if the entire clan was hitching a ride to rest their wings. God was filling my day with his glorious creations.

I stopped paddling and free-floated, content to soak up the sun and relax my mind—but the voice inside my head was like a snake in the grass, slithering silently and then attacking me unaware: *You should be doing something productive. Look at you out here, lollygagging. You are selfish and irresponsible. Why do you think you deserve solitude?* I knew there were things I should be doing instead, like grocery shopping or paying bills or checking in with the restaurant. It felt glorious to spend some quiet time on the lake, but it was hard to do it without feeling guilty.

Paddling slowly back to the cabin, I tried to regain my calm. My anxiety had surfaced, and I considered what our next move should be. The possibilities came at me like darts thrown by a drunken hand—some out in left field and some so near the center of my heart that I felt the pain as real as if the dart tip had pierced me. *When Lacey is found innocent, do we all move far away and begin a new life where no one knows us or our story? Do we move somewhere tropical and take on new identities? Do we trust our daughter's life to a justice system that doesn't seem to be in her favor, or do we take the monetary hit of Lacey skipping bail and hide her away somewhere safe so she doesn't have to stand trial?*

There had been a local case where a family posted bond and the defendant disappeared. He still hadn't been found. I wondered how difficult that would be: to go into hiding and have no contact with your loved ones, always looking over your shoulder for fear of being discovered. Would that be better than prison?

It shocked me that I could consider anything outside of the law. It went against everything I believed. It was there nonetheless. By the time I nudged alongside the mooring, the peaceful solitude I had felt was gone.

chapter 15

MURDER FOR HIRE PLOT
WASHINGTON WOMAN ACCUSED OF
HIRING HIT MAN TO KILL HUSBAND'S
PREGNANT MISTRESS
Lacey Hirst-Pavek is accused of masterminding the plan

I started checking the weekly newspaper's website the evening before the publication would be on the newsstands. If the headline was too inflammatory, I could decide if I wanted to lay low. This one hadn't even said *allegedly*.

It was past noon. I was still in bed. The bedroom blinds were down, the window cranked closed. My eyes felt puffy and were crusted with dried tears from crying myself to sleep. When I rolled out of bed, my knees touched the floor, and I felt compelled to pray. In a childlike pose, with my forearms resting on the mattress and my hands clasped tight together, I raised my eyes toward Heaven and beseeched God, *Lord, please give me guidance. Help me know what to do to help my family and to help myself. Dear God, PLEASE HELP ME.* I closed my eyes and rested my forehead on the duvet.

I'm not sure how long I stayed in prayer position. When I became aware of my surroundings, my legs were needled like I had been there awhile. A warmth bloomed in my heart, and I felt a sense of buoyancy like a balloon floating skyward; I likened the sensibility to when I had accepted Christ at church camp. God was reassuring me that He had heard my prayers.

I went directly to my computer and composed an email. My tears dropped on the keyboard as I typed.

> *Dear friends and family,*
> *I am sending this email to ask for your help and to keep you updated on Lacey's situation. Our first time at court was nerve-racking with Selena's family outnumbering us. I'd like to ask you to come to court with us, if and when you can, to form a protective bubble around Ron, Lacey, and me. I totally understand if you aren't able or choose not to. I cherish your friendship and hope I'm not crossing a fine line here by asking for your help.*
> *I love you all,*
> *Bonnie*
>
> *P.S. I'll email dates and times of the scheduled court appearances.*

At our next court date, Al and Nanc were the first to meet us in the parking lot. As we embraced, my heart swelled with gratitude and tears trickled down my cheeks.

Next to arrive were longtime friends who had known Lacey since she was young. As they hugged her, my heart melted, and more tears fell. Recent friends Ron and I had met while snowmobiling near our cabin—who didn't know Lacey personally—came to bless us with their support. Ron and I took turns greeting each one. Our bubble was heftier than I had hoped for. I felt humbled and honored by their love and willingness to show up for us.

God had answered my prayers tenfold when he guided me to ask our friends for help. It would become the most abundant blessing I would receive throughout this ordeal.

We proceeded inside. A few of Selena's relatives were in the courtroom, but not the entourage that had been there the first time. This court appearance was a formality to waive Lacey's right to a speedy trial and request more time for research and discovery.

MURDER SUSPECT GETS CONTINUANCE

Lacey Hirst-Pavek, who has been charged with seeking the beating of a pregnant Oroville woman, received a continuance of her murder case.

Lacey's trial date would continue to be pushed further into the future by either our lawyer or the prosecutor. Trilby had also wanted to join us in court, to be there for her sister and us, but we didn't want her involved with the justice system or Selena's family, so we'd asked her to not attend. It was bad enough we hadn't been able to protect Lacey. We didn't want to jeopardize her also.

"Mom, if I can't go to court," Trilby asked, "is there something else I can help with?"

"Oh, sweetie, I don't know." Before receiving the blessing of our bubble, my normal reply would have been, "I don't need any help. I've got it covered." Now, though, I asked, "Would you be willing to do the restaurant deposits for me?"

"Are you sure, Mom?" Trilby's eyes widened. "You don't ever ask for help."

"I know, but I'm trying something new for me. Will you help me at the restaurant?"

Trilby not only did the deposits, she also prepared the payroll. I no longer needed to be at the restaurant daily. I had asked for help, and God blessed our mother/daughter bond. It gave me the strength I needed. He was answering my prayers in unanticipated ways.

chapter 16

"Bonnie, I hear rumblings that the prosecutor might ask for the death penalty for the other three who were arrested." Bob, my father-in-law, was on the other end of the line. His voice was shaky. "What if they ask for the death penalty for Lacey?"

A wave of fear leaped through me as I grappled with this new threat. The other three defendants were represented by state-appointed defense attorneys, so their trials were joined. Lacey, with her private attorney, would be tried separately. This was the first time I had thought of all four of them as suspects in the same crime.

Bob had once told me that the grapevine in the county was so fast that he could tell a salesman at his Oroville restaurant a highfalutin story and it would be in the next town within minutes, misconstrued entirely and heavily embellished.

Hoping that was the case here, I tried to waylay his concerns. "I'm sure it's just a rumor, Bob. I can't see the county going to those lengths."

"I hope so Bonnie, but I heard it from a very reliable source."

"This was a drug deal gone bad, and Lacey is their scapegoat," I said. "It's all going to work out okay."

The phone call left me weak-kneed. My father-in-law had been a county commissioner a few years back and had sources inside the courthouse. Could there be some truth to this? Before that moment, I had believed that Lacey's charges would be miraculously dropped when they realized she wasn't an accomplice to Selena's death.

⁕⁖⁖⁖⁕

PROSECUTOR SEEKS ELEVATED CHARGES
3 of 4 people charged with murdering a pregnant woman will appear in court to hear if charges against them will be elevated.

Before Lacey's arrest, I was not one of those women who nested in their bedroom. My bed now became my sanctuary. Buried under the covers, I felt cordoned off from the ugliness of the outside world. *If I could just stay in this cocoon, I'd be okay,* I thought, but the minute my eyes closed, my mind would whiz off into things-that-need-to-be-done mode. The shelter I sought became my torment instead. My mind seldom stopped asking questions: *What went wrong? How could I have prevented this? What is my role now?*

In my self-help library, one book suggested creating a mantra to calm anxiety. I tried out several variations and finally settled on this: *My family and I are safe, protected, and very blessed.*

As I said *safe*, I would picture my mom's arms from heaven wrapping warmly around me. She had lost her fight with breast cancer twenty years earlier. On the word *protected*, I envisioned a steadfast realm of guardian angels watching over us; and on *very blessed*, I visualized God answering my prayers. In this way, I summoned all the heavenly help known to me.

I printed little placards with pictures of angels framing my mantra and put one in my car, one on my bathroom mirror, and one in a frame on my kitchen counter. I gave one to Lacey, Danny, Blaine, and Meri. I asked them to recite it often.

Most days I could feel God and my angels' presence, but on down days, I felt as if I were climbing a steep mountain, carefully grasping at each foothold or handhold, inching my way out of despair through prayer. Sometimes my faith eluded me, and before I could reach the top, I would slide back down into my pit of worry. Was I able or even willing to crawl back up? Some days not. Some days I just needed to be alone with my worries. To sort them out, or not. To get out of bed, or not.

chapter 17

CHARGES AMENDED FOR TRIO
DEATH PENALTY NOT ADDED
3 of 4 people charged with murdering a pregnant
woman who was 11 weeks pregnant, won't face the
death penalty if found guilty

Our home phone seemed to take on a life of its own, with echoes, strange clicking sounds, and long pauses. Long-distance calls to my sister and my dad had the most static. I cautioned them to not ask detailed questions because I was concerned that our phone conversations were being recorded. I felt like Will Smith's character in *Enemy of the State*, where the government tracks his every move. We didn't have anything to hide, but that hadn't stopped them from arresting Lacey. She had offered her phone records and her bank records. She had told them about Carly's threat. All of it had then been construed to make her look guilty. Heaven forbid the prosecutor recorded our phone conversations and twisted them into something they weren't.

Trilby's house sits a couple hundred yards west of ours. One day she watched a pale blue cargo van steer cautiously up the lane. It made a U-turn near Lacey's trailer, then stopped. A muscular guy lifted the hood of the van and pretended to pour the contents of a gallon jug into the radiator. Rubbernecking, he scanned our house, the shop, Lacey's trailer, and Trilby's house. When he saw Trilby watching from her kitchen window, he slammed the hood and sped away.

The man and his van fit the description of a local thug in the area. Was he here to steal something, or to harm Lacey? What if he hadn't seen Trilby watching him? Lacey had been asleep in her trailer at the time, and unaware of his approach. Would she have been able to protect herself if he'd attempted anything?

Ron purchased a long-range driveway sensor that would warn us if anyone approached. We also gave each daughter a receiver that doubled as a walkie-talkie. When the sensor was triggered, a programmed female voice announced, *"Alert Zone One. Alert Zone Two."* When someone left, it alarmed in reverse: *"Alert Zone Two. Alert Zone One."* It made me feel a bit safer, but the singsong voice was also a stark reminder of why we needed to be aware in the first place.

When the alarm sounded in the middle of the night, *"Alert Zone One,"* I'd awaken and listen for the next warning. Had it been a deer traveling to the alfalfa field across the road, or was someone advancing up the drive? If the sensor sounded again, I'd worry that two vehicles were converging to do us harm. I had Ron to protect me, but Lacey was alone.

Returning to sleep was impossible after such a wakeup, so I wandered through our darkened house, keeping a keen eye out the window toward Lacey's trailer. *Dear Lord, keep us safe and protected.*

<hr />

With Lacey in limbo, our round oak dining table became the center for family Monopoly games. Trilby joined us with her two-year-old daughter, Rylee, and along with both of Lacey's kids, Blaine and Meri, we rolled the dice and moved around the vintage board purchasing property, little green houses, and large red hotels. The dice edges were rounded from years of use, the Chance and Community Chest cards were dog-eared, and the colorful money had faded. When Lacey and Trilby were little, they had used the fake bills in their make-believe stores.

When my mom was alive, our family often played cards around the kitchen table. Ten Point Pitch was my favorite. Mom always had a candy dish filled to the brim with Peanut M&M's, and its contents emptied as we played. Mirroring her tradition, I kept a bag on hand during these game nights. As my girls and grandkids popped the colored morsels into their mouths and played Monopoly, it seemed the outside world disappeared, and with it all of our troubles.

"It's your turn, Lacey," I said during one such evening.

Lacey rolled the dice. "Dammit, I'm in jail again," she said as she counted the squares. It was her fourth time landing on the corner with the jail bars.

The first and second time, I had joked with her, "At least you can't buy up any more property in there." She had accumulated more real estate than the rest of us. The third time, Trilby had quickly rolled the dice to remove the attention from her sister. This fourth time, a hush settled over the table. It was as if we didn't acknowledge her actual jail time, we could pretend it hadn't happened.

For Lacey to have something to fill her days, we planted a garden. We'd always had a garden plot until we moved to this acreage, where the sandy soil wasn't very good for growing vegetables. Ron hauled in topsoil and cow manure and then built a tall wire fence to keep the deer from foraging on the new vegetation. Lacey planted cilantro, jalapeño peppers, Roma tomatoes, and green onions—the makings for her fresh homemade salsa. Rows of corn flourished in the summer heat, surrounded by pumpkins, watermelons, cucumbers, radishes, cherry tomatoes, and carrots. The lush green garden became our private countryside preserve. We delighted in the zesty aroma of the cilantro, the peppery taste of the radishes, the prickliness of the cucumber vines, and the spicy residue on the jalapeno's skin; we were handing down traditions of harvesting as a family. The corn stalks tasseled out in mid-August when the ears were ready, and it wasn't long before we were sharing the extra bounty with our friends.

Working in the garden felt like being in a time warp. Daytime worry over Lacey's situation would build and then give way in the cool of the evening as we came together to care for our plants. Trilby and her family joined us as we popped ripe cherry tomatoes into our mouths and took turns pulling weeds. We looked like an ordinary family carrying on daily rituals.

Thank You, Lord, for watching over my family. Thank You for our good health, our abundant love, and for being there for me. Thank You for giving me comfort. I also asked Him for His grace toward any new challenges that were yet to come.

chapter 18

Summer turned into fall, and Ron spent an increasing amount of time at our cabin to help our friends Steve and Dena remodel an old house nearby. For me, the solitude at home felt like a gift. I didn't have to worry about doing anything for anyone else. No dinners to make, no laundry, no cleaning. I could read a book and disappear into its pages for hours.

When Ron and I did share the same space, we seldom talked about what was foremost in our minds: *What if Lacey is convicted? What if our businesses suffer from the fallout? What if our family is so fractured we don't survive?* To ask those questions out loud would beg for answers.

On the weekends, when Lacey's kids came to stay with her, I would travel to the cabin, kayak a bit, and then join Ron at Steve and Dena's, where there was always lots of food and libation. Dena's genuine love of everyone was expressed in her enthusiastic greetings, huge hugs, and sincere concern. I always felt nurtured in her presence. She and Steve were instrumental in helping Ron survive this trying time.

After dinner, we would join our cabin community at karaoke. In the darkened bar, Ron sang Elvis Presley songs—a foray into public singing that surprised me. When we dated in high school, he was the proverbial wallflower at dances, never joining in, never bringing attention to himself. Now his baritone voice resonated deep within me. As he sang "I Can't Help Falling in Love with You" his eyes coupled with mine, and my heart delighted in this man I had married so long ago. Tears filled my eyes as I soaked up the love he sent to me in song. My girlfriends swooned and wished their men would sing to them. They weren't aware that Ron serenading me in front of a bar full of people was essentially our only communication during this time. I would return home Sunday afternoon and know that at the end of the week, he would open his heart to me again. It was as if he could harmonize his love but wasn't able to voice it aloud.

There were times when not having his verbal or physical closeness was like a jolt of pain to my heart. For example, when we sat in court during one pretrial appearance, I rested my hand on his thigh, seeking connection. He brushed it off. I scooted closer to him, and he inched away. I felt trampled and confused.

On the drive home I asked, "Why don't you want to be close to me?"

"Because I can feel your pain," he said, "and it's too much for me to handle."

I keeled into myself as if I'd been pierced with a flaming arrow and part of me had been incinerated. How could I cope without him?

I understood what he meant, sort of. I felt the same way with my friends Dena and Elaine. Their empathy when we were one-on-one gave me sustenance. They each responded with a wellspring of tenderness. But in court, sitting next to them, their concern encased me, and my eyes would mist up. I hadn't realized that I poured pain onto Ron the same way.

From then on, I was cognizant of the space between us on the courtroom bench. I encouraged Nanc to sit on my other side. She was my rock. Our minds worked alike as we observed the legal proceedings. Nanc noticed subtle body language and had an awareness of her surroundings that I came to rely on.

Toward the end of the trial—the night before we were to hear the verdict—I asked Ron if he would make an exception and hold my hand the following day. I needed his familiarity. He acquiesced. God's guidance for me to ask for help came through again. I don't know what I would have done without Ron to hold on to when they pronounced Lacey guilty.

* * * * *

On those weekends at the cabin, listening to karaoke, I drank until the alcohol numbed my senses. The bar served oversized glasses of wine. Merlot was my drink of choice. Most any brand would do, but Australian grapes were my favorite. It helped me push the outside world to the back of the shelf. In my tipsiness, I could just be me—not Lacey's mom, or a business owner, or the bill payer. I could be Bonnie. I could fall into bed with the perpetual swirling motion of my drunkenness and pass out until the morning sun rose high in the mountain sky.

If the lake was calm, I'd kayak. If not, I'd watch the hummingbirds flit between my two red feeders and the towering pine trees. Many times, the tiny birds hovered directly in front of me, their tails undulating and their high-pitched chirps communicating with me. I inherited my love of hummingbirds from my mom. She always had feeders for the tiny creatures, and her face would light up when they appeared. The buzzy trill of their wings and the way they zip backward and sideways bring my soul peace. It's like my mom has arrived, and I can feel her love surrounding me. She is saying, "I am with you, dear Bonnie."

Lacey's trial date had been rescheduled for October but was postponed again. Relieved that we had more time, I also grew increasingly apprehensive. The unknown hung over me like a tornado funnel in the distance. I didn't know where or how violently it might touch down. I cleaned closets, junk drawers, and file cabinets. By organizing unseen chaos, I attempted to regain order in my life.

When the karaoke bar burned down that year, my over-imbibing every weekend came to a halt.

It seemed not a week went by without Lacey's mug shot being brandished on the front page with the other three defendants. Plastered side by side, four sets of beady eyes—my daughter's appearing the most disturbed—accosted me from newspaper boxes around town. The tiny gas station where I filled up weekly had a stack of papers just inside its front door. The blaring murder headlines would bushwhack my sensibilities each time I entered. It was like driving by the scene of an accident: you look to see if it's anyone you know before you go on past—and it turns out to be your daughter.

I often perused these articles without buying the paper, but if it were continued on an interior page, I'd pick it up, fold it onto itself so I couldn't see Lacey's mug shot, and purchase it along with my gas. Arriving home, I'd park in the garage and prop the pages over the steering wheel to read it, as if not taking it into the house would keep the distortions from entering our lives.

Lacey and I were sitting on the front porch one evening watching the sun set. "It seems to me, Mom," she said, "that your friends are the only ones that even come near me."

"I'm sorry, sweetie, that your friends have deserted you, but you've still got me." I wiggled my eyebrows at her like Groucho Marx would do, trying to lighten her mood. "I may be your mom, but I can also be your best friend."

"Yeah, but as my mom, I can't really tell you how much I miss Danny, since you don't care for him and what he's done."

"You've got a point there," I said. "But as a best friend, I could try to put that judgment aside and just be a shoulder for you to lean on."

Lacey's eyes overflowed. "Oh, Mom, I would appreciate that."

chapter 19

Hesitancy invaded my body when Lacey wanted to plant garlic that September. In our climate, garlic is planted in the fall and harvested the following summer. Lacey's trial was scheduled for February. Would my prayers be strong enough for Lacey to be declared innocent? If not, would I be digging the garlic up alone? Would the bulbs rot in the ground if she wasn't here for harvest?

I didn't share my doubts with Lacey. Instead, I trusted God to have put it upon her heart that she would be here to reap the rewards the following summer. A local co-op helped us choose three varieties: a Purple Stripe Chesnok Red that was easy to peel and great for cooking, a Hardneck Killarney Red, and an Idaho Silver Silverskin that was perfect for braiding. Side by side in the garden, Lacey and I nestled the bulbs into place following a planting guide. The earthy scent of the mulched soil brought a quietude to my soul, and I knew God was with us as we completed our task. He would provide.

Thanksgiving arrived, and I invited Ron's dad and stepmom, his mom and stepdad, Trilby's family, Ron's brother and his family, and Lacey, Blaine, and Meri. Ron and I elongated the oak table by adding three extra leaves. Meri helped me spread an embroidered tablecloth over its mass, and we graced it with autumn leaves, harvest-colored napkins, and my mom's china. Everything appeared perfect. The comforting aroma of roasted turkey greeted our guests as they arrived but did little to assuage my nerves. I appeared calm, but inside I had whipped my worries into nail-biting uneasiness that someone would mention Lacey's arrest or the latest headlines and Lacey would become uncomfortable.

I needn't have worried. Family love floated in the air, and even though the turkey was overcooked, cornstarch lumps floated in the gravy, and I forgot the cranberry sauce, my vision of a Norman Rockwell Thanksgiving was sealed. Our family had gathered with thankful hearts.

Asking everyone to join hands in prayer, I began, "Our gracious heavenly Father. . . ." Then my voice wavered, and my throat constricted. My tears flowed freely with gratitude for the day and for the people seated at my table. The supplication I had written and rehearsed went unfinished. Ron covered for me with the familiar, "God is great, God is good, let us thank Him for this food." A resounding "Amen" circled the table.

Lacey and I orchestrated a family game day for Christmas. With our family ranging from three years of age to eighty-six and Ron's stepdad in the beginning stages of dementia, we chose simple options. Separating into small groups, we played Barrel of Monkeys, connecting one blue monkey arm to another curled tail. On the raised counter, the Operation board buzzed, and the red nose flashed when the tweezers touched the metal cavity. Trilby's little one, Rylee, loved making the buzzer go off. She'd giggle and set if off again. Buzz, buzz. The tower-building game of Jenga, with its rectangular wooden blocks, clattered when it collapsed onto the table. The impact left small divots on the oak surface that are still visible today. Ron's dad kept intentionally making the blocks fall just to hear his great-grandkids laugh. It was a joy-filled day, and I sent up thanks to God.

Winter descended on us. The water lines froze in the travel trailer, and Lacey moved into our spare bedroom. Danny left to spend time with his grandpa in Montana. Blaine and Meri also moved in with us. It felt God-sent having them under our roof again.

chapter 20

Lacey's trial was to start in February 2010, and she wanted to protect her kids from what might be printed in the papers or decided upon in court during the proceedings. I volunteered to drive them eight hundred miles to the small town where Danny was staying with his grandfather. Lacey's bail restraints didn't allow her to leave the county. Part of me wanted to keep Blaine and Meri close, at home with us, but I also needed to be with Lacey in court.

There had been the usual late-January thaw in the valley. Our driveway was muddy and lined with remnants of snow where Ron had plowed. The morning we were to leave, Lacey hugged her sleepy son and daughter, fastened their seatbelts, and kissed them each on the cheek. As I chauffeured them away, I watched in the rearview mirror as Ron pulled Lacey close, and I saw her shoulders heave up and down as she sobbed. My eyes became faucets as I drove Blaine and Meri away from their mom.

Blaine looked at me and asked, "You okay, Grandma?"

"I will be in a moment, bud," I said as I wiped my tears.

Before I pulled onto the highway, I looked at Lacey's children and wondered if their young minds were alert to the menacing circumstances that had become a part of their lives.

Were they just holding their feelings in? Or were they blissfully unaware of the emotional trauma their mom had just experienced as she let them go? I sent up prayers for safe travels and my family's protection.

"Okay," I said, trying to sound cheerful, "there are some new movies in the pouch on the back of the seat, and your Mom packed snacks and lunch."

I hoped to cover six hundred miles the first day; the forecast called for snow at higher elevations. Meri turned on the DVD player, snuggled into her pillow and fleece blanket, and began to watch *Shrek*. Blaine reclined the front passenger seat and closed his eyes. It wasn't long before they were both asleep. I drove for several hours with the soundtrack of *Shrek* in the background.

*　＊　＊　＊　＊　＊*

When I was ready to stop for the night, I chose a tremendous log-structured motel that boasted a large pool and five hot tubs. Entering the lobby, we were encompassed in a lush green canopy of evergreen trees. Rock outcroppings with waterfalls formed a mountainous sanctuary in the middle of the three-story lodge. I ordered pizza, and we headed to the swimming pool.

There was a young girl about Meri's age in the pool; the two girls immediately befriended one another, and they swam and splashed in the shallows while Blaine and I swam the length of the pool.

"Let's race," he challenged.

"Okay," I said, and immediately pushed off from the shallow end.

My crawl stroke, perfected after years on the swim team, won the race. Afterward, I demonstrated an underwater turn and instructed Blaine on how to gauge the distance to the end of the pool. I succeeded in boring him. He swam over to join the girls.

I climbed out of the pool and dipped into a hot tub. My tense shoulder muscles relaxed in the jetted hot water, but my mind deflected to Lacey and the upcoming trial. *God, please watch over her. Watch over all of my family and help me safely deliver Blaine and Meri to Danny and return in time for the trial.* Again, I wondered if the kids fully grasped why I was taking them to spend time with Danny and his grandpa. Was it my place to explain their mother's situation to them? If not, whose was it?

That evening, a DVD playing and pizza strewn on the bedside table, I stretched out on one bed and fell asleep. I awoke later to the buzz of the blinking TV screen. Both kids were asleep on top of the covers on the other bed. Their skinny arms were splayed at funny angles, like they had just flopped to a supine position. I draped my bedspread gently over them. I scolded myself, feeling like I had let my grandkids down by going to sleep first. I should have snuggled with them as they watched the movie. I should have interacted with them into the emergent hours of the morning. I should have asked if they had any questions about leaving their mom. I should have reassured them that all would be well.

In the top drawer of the nightstand, I found the customary Bible and pressed it to my heart, seeking comfort. Needing more sleep, I laid it on the pillow next to me, then reached for it and splayed it open. Maybe God would best hear my prayers with His scriptures revealed as I slept.

The next morning, Blaine roused first and climbed onto my bed, nudging me to wake up. Picking up the open Bible, he asked, "Why is this on the bed?"

"It calms me," I told him.

"We should get Mom one," he said.

I didn't know then that a few months earlier, Lacey had purchased an English Standard Version Bible. Later, I would find the inscription she wrote on the inside: *I found Christ – September 2, 2009. I kept getting a nagging saying to purchase a Bible, read, and think, and ask questions. Now I can truly say I put my life into God's hands. I feel at home when I pray, and when I have a bad day I can feel him grab me by the scruff of my neck, pick me up, and put me back on the chair of faith. I hope someday my husband can find what I have. Peace amid chaos.*

After traveling a few more hours that day, I delivered Blaine and Meri to Danny. I then drove steadfastly home—only to learn soon after my return that my trip had been a waste. Lacey's trial had been postponed again. It would be another eight months before she would go to trial. Either Haney or the prosecutor kept asking for a continuance, and the date just kept getting pushed further out. It seemed like our lives would be on hold forever.

With the trial postponed and Danny and the kids in Montana, Lacey decided to return to her house.

"Lacey, I don't think this is a good idea," I said, as I leaned against the doorjamb of the spare bedroom. She had just finished stuffing her clothes into a plastic garbage sack.

"I knew you wouldn't like it, Mom, me being out there alone, but I need to be in my own house." She looked toward me as she placed a framed family portrait on top of her clothes. "When Danny brings the kids home in a couple of weeks, his mom says he's going to stay at a friend's house, so I can have the kids with me twenty-four-seven."

"Sweetie, what if Carly still has someone after you?" I folded my arms across my ribs, and my foot began to jig. "How can you feel safe out there?"

"I'll be fine, Mom. I've encroached on you and Dad long enough." She hoisted the bag with both arms, like a football player practicing tackles. "I need to do this for me."

I wanted to block her exit, to wedge my body into the doorjamb and not allow her passage, but I knew she wasn't about to change her mind. Instead, I kissed the side of her cheek and watched her leave.

My house was empty once again.

Danny spent a few weeks in town after bringing the kids home, then returned to his grandpa's in Montana. Blaine had friends over that weekend for his thirteenth birthday. The kids were shooting airsoft guns out the window when a town police car came barreling down the drive with lights flashing. Lacey told me the boys cowered in the bedroom as the officers besieged the front porch in search of Danny. They were sure he would be there for Blaine's birthday. Lacey met them at the door and convinced them Danny wasn't there. That would have been a breach of her bail requirements, and they would have been able to arrest her on the spot.

After the cops retreated, Lacey called me, and her fevered voice recounted the scene. She was sobbing by the end, horrified that Blaine's friends had witnessed the drama.

Enraged at the cops' intrusion, I sped to city hall, blathering aloud in my car what I would say to the officers when I found them.

They were standing in the lobby when I stormed in.

"You just attacked my daughter's house knowing full well it was her son's birthday. What kind of monsters are you people? Do you not have any boundaries?" My pitch increased. "My grandkids have had enough shit thrown at them after Lacey's arrest, they don't need you adding to it." I looked from one cop to the other. "How would you feel if someone did that to your kids?" I shook my head back and forth then spat out, "How dare you!"

I didn't wait for a response. I harrumphed back to my car. My hands shook uncontrollably as I drove to Lacey's.

chapter 21

TAXMAN PLEADS GUILTY, WILL TESTIFY
A Spokane man pleaded guilty to murder Monday and
agreed to testify against three others who authorities say
were involved in a jealous wife's murder-for-hire plot.

The taxman's original prison sentence, without a plea deal, would have been life without parole. Agreeing to testify brought it down to twenty-six years. His graphic testimony during Carly's trial included emboldened details of the murder and underscored the machinations of the drug world.

JURY CONVICTS TWO IN MURDER OF PREGNANT WOMAN

The jury returned verdicts at 11 pm Thursday. Carly Reeves was found guilty of aggravated murder of Selena Clark, manslaughter of her unborn child, kidnapping, and tampering with evidence. She will be sentenced to life in prison without parole. The prosecutor did not seek the death penalty. Mark Peterson was found guilty of second-degree murder and manslaughter. Investigators say Lacey Hirst-Pavek planned the attack because Clark was having an affair with her husband, who was the father of Clark's baby. Hirst-Pavek is scheduled for trial later this year.

After Carly's conviction, Danny was allowed to move back home with Lacey, since he hadn't testified against the other defendants. I was thankful for the blessing that allowed her and my grandkids to return to a semblance of a normal life before the trial. I continued to send up prayers for protection for her and her family.

I sent this email to our bubble:

We have a court date next Thursday. The prosecutor is requesting to increase Lacey's charge to aggravated murder. He may also seek to have her bail revoked, which would land her in jail until her trial. This would be devastating to her kids. We would appreciate your positive energy that morning. Thank you in advance for your prayers. Love, Bonnie and Ron

In the courtroom, surrounded by our bubble, we listened as the judge ruled to accept the increased charge. This should have sent fear through us, given we'd just seen how Carly's trial had turned out. But we were more concerned about the prosecutor seeking revocation of her bail. When he didn't ask the judge to send Lacey back to jail, I knew God and my angels were in the room.

An email from my friend Elaine echoed our relief:

Bonnie,

You and Ron are awesome. You are on some other spiritual plane that I can barely glimpse. Your strengths and goodnesses are very present. I thank you for the privilege of allowing me to share in your lives. That moment today when the judge asked the prosecutor if there was anything else, receiving the answer, "No, Your Honor," will stay with me a long time. I felt the walls move outward and joy at walking out of the building with you, Lacey, and the others.

Love, Elaine

<hr />

CHARGES STIFFENED IN STABBING DEATH

Lacey Hirst-Pavek, 35, is now charged with aggravated first-degree murder and faces a mandatory life sentence if convicted. She had been charged with first-degree murder and would have faced a maximum of 26 years in prison if found guilty. Hirst-Pavek showed no visible emotion after the judge's ruling.

After the publicity of Carly's trial, we sought a change of venue for Lacey. Haney said we needed letters from non-family members to show the judge how the publicity about Lacey during Carly's trial had tainted any possible local jury pool. Friends who worked at the post office, Walmart, the hospital, and a clothing store gave examples of the gossip they'd overheard during Carly's trial and how even though Lacey wasn't on trial at the time, they'd heard her name often. They all doubted Lacey would get a fair trial if it stayed in the county.

This is the letter I wrote:

I am Lacey Hirst-Pavek's mother. As I read the local newspapers, watch the TV, listen to the radio, or go online to read the news, my daughter's name and mug shot are matched with bold headlines. This has been the scenario for over a year now. Since there were four defendants in the case, it seemed there was something new to be printed almost weekly. During and after the codefendants' trial in April, the publicity got even worse. It's not just the written news reports or the radio or the TV or blog posts with a "Hate Lacey" fan club, it's also the word of mouth grapevine that all small communities have.

In the codefendants' trial, testimony against Lacey ran rampant. Newspaper articles (printed and online) shared that testimony with readers. In a small community such as this, the grapevine gets very active. The consensus is very negative and loud against my daughter. There are always two sides to every story, and my daughter's story has yet to be told. In our country, a person is supposed to be innocent until proven guilty. In small communities, such as ours, one is innocent until an article is printed in the local newspaper.

My heart aches. I believe our county has already made up its mind and my daughter will not get a fair trial here. I respectfully request a change of venue for Lacey's trial.
Sincerely,
Bonnie S. Hirst

Writing that letter, I believed God had guided my hand, and that all would work out for the best. All would be well again.

HIRST-PAVEK WINS VENUE CHANGE
*The final defendant accused in last year's slaying of a
pregnant Oroville woman will face a Nov 1 jury trial
in a different county*

Winning the change of venue felt like things were evolv-
ing in our favor. The win solidified my belief that God was
answering my prayers.

chapter 22

We had a bit of a reprieve that summer from court dates and newspaper headlines, except for the impending November trial date. It was like being diagnosed with an illness, and you wait and wait for future doctor appointments to know if your treatments are working. My treatments were my prayers. Would God answer them and vindicate my daughter? I believed He would.

Ron and I spent much of that summer at the cabin. He helped Steve and Dena finish remodeling the old house, and I whiled away the hours on the lake in my kayak. One day I took my camera and photographed turtles resting on logs and baby ducks amid the green rushes next to the shore. The photos were my attempt to capture the harmonious aura of the lake. I framed them in rustic wood and created a collage on the kitchen wall at the cabin. At first, the pictures of the billowing green reeds, the fuzziness of the ducklings, and the orange edging on the turtle's shells all lulled me into a peaceful state. Now they just remind me of the summer before Lacey went to prison.

Ron's stepdad passed away that August. I was in Canada visiting my sister when I got the call. The anguish in Ron's voice ripped me open. "I'm so sorry, honey," I said. My sister's arm hugged my shoulder. I'm sure I asked lots of questions. I don't remember Ron being emotionally able to answer them. It felt wrong that I had the comfort of my sister and Ron was home alone.

Pat had raised Ron. Together they'd logged hours and hours hiking rough terrain in search of wild game. He had mentored the man I'd married to be kind, thoughtful, and forthright in all endeavors. Pat's legacy of straightforward honesty had influenced many.

When I arrived home a few days later, Ron was in his recliner. The haunted look he gave me conveyed, *Please don't ask any more questions.* I sat on the overstuffed armrest and leaned in to kiss his forehead.

His head moved slowly side to side. "I never understood what you went through when your mom died." Through choked sobs, he said, "I can't take any more pain."

I held him as we both cried.

The infinite emptiness we feel when a loved one dies is all-consuming. It is hard to believe the grief will ever go away. Mom died in 1995. I still miss her, but that pain has softened into loving memories. I often feel her presence as her angel wings watch over me. I'm sure Pat is up there now, watching over Ron.

The garlic we'd planted in the fall became robust stalks ready for harvest. Lacey and I pulled the plants from the soil and filled empty onion sacks with each variety. God had come through once again. Lacey took the garlic home and hung the sacks from the rafters of her porch. Later, when they were dry, she filled lunch-sized brown paper bags, neatly folded, stapled, and labeled with a black marker in her lefty writing. Half the harvest, she shared with me, and I stocked two rows of the aromatic bags in my pantry.

Late fall is also the time we search the forest for shaggy mane mushrooms. The weather has to be just right: a little rain, a light frost, and the delicate shrooms seem to pop up overnight. We have been gathering the elusive shaggy for years. Ron's dad would congregate the family each fall, and together we'd walk the roadsides as Bob leapfrogged his white Suburban ahead of us. Shaggys are easily identified by their tall bullet shape and wispy shags on the outside.

A month before Lacey's trial, Mother Nature cooperated with perfect conditions. Trilby, Lacey, Meri, Rylee, and I combed the forest floor on a beautiful fall day. The sun was bright. The aspen leaves had turned gold. Chipmunks skittered up pine trees. Birds trilled their songs. The radio was tuned to rock music, at Lacey's request, and the girls sang along to "Born in the USA" with Bruce Springsteen. I had packed sandwiches, Kool-Aid, and cookies in anticipation of picnicking in the woods.

Laughter was abundant as we combed the forest floor, hunting shaggys like they were Easter eggs. With all of my girls together, the sun appeared brighter, the chorus of birds seemed more melodious, and the golden sunbeams angling from heaven radiated with an intensity I'd never witnessed. With every laugh we shared, and each mushroom we plucked, I told myself, *Latch on to this memory and store this joy in your heart.*

chapter 23

Lacey felt Haney wasn't giving 100 percent, so we retained a second attorney. Tad Rockwell knew our family and took a personal interest in Lacey's case. We believed he would fight for Lacey's innocence. A week before trial, Ron, Lacey, and I met with both attorneys. We were seated around a large conference table in Tad's office. The polished surface was covered with documents, files, pens, and Styrofoam coffee cups. I twisted one of Tad's fancy bronze pens open and closed.

Tad began the meeting. "Lacey, I think you should ask for a forty-year plea deal. After watching Carly's trial and seeing her outcome, I—"

"I can't bring myself to plead guilty to something I didn't do," Lacey said before he could continue. "Tad, what kind of message does that send to my kids?"

"But, Lacey—"

"I can't, Tad. Forty years? I'll be seventy-five. My kids will be over fifty. I'll miss all of their birthdays, graduations, weddings."

Tad softened his voice. "Lacey, are you willing to go to prison for life for the sake of your principles? Look at how Carly's trial turned out."

Neither option was good. Looking at Ron sitting next to me, I projected us forty years into the future. We would be in our late nineties. Would we still be alive when Lacey got out? What if she got convicted and received life? She would die there. Visions of grandbabies Lacey would never be able to hold wilted my heart.

"Dad, Mom, what do you think I should do?"

Ron answered for both of us. "Lacey, this is not a decision we can make for you."

My husband is thoughtful and reasoned in any situation. He sees the broad spectrum and arrives at rational conclusions. When he chooses to speak, I defer to his judgment. We had come to this meeting thinking it was to learn what the joint approach would be for Lacey's defense. Now, I felt like our lawyers wanted to surrender Lacey to the wolves.

When we left the meeting, I hugged Lacey. "Sweetie, I'll pray and ask God to give you guidance."

"I'll ask Him for help too," Lacey said.

I held her at arm's length and quizzed her with my eyes.

"I've been reading the Bible, Mom," she said. "It gives me peace."

Lacey's words warmed my heart. Surely, now that we were both trusting God for the best outcome, He would answer our prayers twofold. That evening, I struggled with how to ask God to grant a plea deal. How could I ask Him to send Lacey to prison, even for a short time? If I asked for that, was I signaling to Him that I didn't trust Him to bring about the highest good for my daughter? Was I short-circuiting His plan for our lives?

Lacey also struggled many hours considering the pros and cons of a plea. The next day, she had Tad present an option of a twenty-five-year plea deal to the prosecutor. With good behavior, she could be out sooner than that.

"Why did you decide that?" I asked.

"Think about it, Mom," she said. "If the answer is no, then I go to trial with the knowledge that God's highest good does not include a plea deal."

I was surprised that Lacey would even consider a plea. She had always stood up for what she believed was right. Once, during high school, a history teacher told Lacey's class that if they didn't register to vote, they wouldn't pass his class. Lacey got her back up and said that wasn't legal. She researched the Revised Code of Washington on student's rights, presented her findings to the superintendent, and he directed the teacher to pull the voting requirement. Lacey hadn't registered to vote that year even though her grandfather was up for election for county commissioner. She'd held to her principles.

I believed asking for a plea deal went against her moral standards, but I wasn't the one who had been handcuffed, searched, and put in jail. That has to change your mental acuity.

The prosecutor said no to the plea arrangement.

⁕—⁕—⁕—⁕—⁕

It happened that the trial would be moved near to where Al and Nanc lived. With their insistence, during the trial, Ron and I would settle into their spare bedroom. We would park our travel trailer in their shop for Lacey to have a quiet place to stay. The proximity to the courtroom without needing to rent a motel room was a godsend, and I accepted it as another prayer answered.

The Friday before trial, Lacey stopped by the house, her backseat overflowing with groceries. "Did you go a little overboard, sweetie?" I asked.

"Probably. I just wanted Danny and the kids to have food while I'm away for trial the next two weeks." She cleared her throat, trying not to cry. Sorting through the bags, she handed me one with perishable items to put into the travel trailer.

"Hmm," I said as I looked inside. "Chocolate milk, pizza, ice cream, cookie dough. Think you have enough comfort food?" My mind went back to the first time I had received an unbaked roll of Toll House chocolate chip cookie dough. Mom had sent me a care package at church camp with the bright-yellow plastic tube of raw dough, along with eight plastic spoons so I could share with my cabin mates. I still remember all of us gathered on my bunk, scooping out as much dough as possible on our turn. The dull beam of a flashlight shone on the tube itself, and as each camper swallowed the chocolaty sweetness, I heard oohs and aahs in the dark.

I had shared Mom's tradition with Lacey when she was at cheer camp. She said she became the favorite girl that day as she shared the sweet dough with her friends.

"I'm hoping I won't need the comfort because the trial will go my way," Lacey said. "But I intend to be prepared." As she looked at me, her face crumpled.

I placed the bag I was holding on the ground and gathered her into my arms. "Do you remember our conversation about friend versus mother?"

"Yeah, I remember." She wiped her tears on her sleeve. "Why?"

I kissed her cheek. "Which one do you need me to be during the trial: your mother or your friend?"

"Oh, Mom." Lacey wept as she hugged me. "I need both."

Ron and I were at the kitchen table having coffee. We usually watch *Good Morning America* in our recliners, but today we had gravitated to the dining nook.

"Yesterday, as I was driving home," Ron said, "my mind was running what-if scenarios. And then, suddenly, it was like I didn't need to run them anymore, because I felt that everything was going to be all right."

It surprised and comforted me that Ron had received and was sharing positive thoughts with me. I don't often know what he feels, since he keeps everything close to the vest; of course, that could be because I'm always guiding the conversations and seldom wait or ask for input. But on this day, he voiced what I was also experiencing.

"I know, hon. Me too," I said. "It feels weird to be calm."

———※———※———※———※———

Sunday evening, we drove the two hours to Al and Nanc's. A slow-cooked stew was simmering on the stove, and the house smelled like my childhood Sundays.

Gathered in the kitchen, we skirted the trial topic until it was time to retire.

"Lacey, is it okay if Al and I attend the jury selection tomorrow?" Nanc asked.

Lacey had suggested that our bubble wait until the actual trial before they joined us.

"Absolutely," Lacey answered.

———※———※———※———※———

Fifty-six prospective jurors filled the small courtroom and were instructed to fill out a nineteen-page questionnaire. The usual hardship cases were excused. Lacey and her attorneys took notes while Nanc, Ron, Al, and I tried to be invisible in the back of the courtroom. Writing down juror numbers, I drew smiley faces next to those I got an immediate fuzzy warmth from, frowny faces for those who looked judgmental, minus signs for jurors I thought the prosecutor might like, and plus signs for ones we might want. I described what they wore—dusty cowboy boots, lime green plastic clogs, Nike running shoes, black oxfords, silky animal print blouse, faded blue chambray shirt, zippered purple sweatshirt, crinkly black windbreaker—and how they looked: chin goatee, long narrow face, shiny face, pocked face, long stringy hair, gray hair and full beard, horn-rimmed glasses. I put a checkmark next to each of the twenty-one of the fifty-six potential jurors who admitted they had heard about the case even though we had moved the trial one hundred miles away.

The final jury of twelve consisted of eight men and four women. Of those twelve, I had marked four with smiley faces. There were none that I had marked with a frowny face. Selected jurors ranged in age from thirty to seventy. Overall, Lacey and I felt confident about the group.

⚜

On the first morning of the trial, a gleaming rainbow stretched across the cloudless sky. I took a picture of Lacey as the translucent colors arched around her. For me, that rainbow held a promise that God was there with us. As we drove the ten minutes from Nanc's to the courthouse, the reassuring band of colors seemed to follow us.

Above the third-floor landing, in a small meeting room, Ron, Lacey, and I joined Haney and Tad before the trial started. The court clerk had ushered us there so we wouldn't run into Selena's family as they arrived. The air in the room was stagnant from lack of circulation, the windows painted shut, and the sills dusty. From our vantage point, we could see the parking lot, the wooden stairwell, and the dimpled glass of the courtroom door. We saw our bubble arrive and watched as Nanc ushered them inside. Several people we didn't recognize, along with Selena's family, also entered the courtroom. The clock was nearing 9:00 a.m. Court would convene soon.

The actual trial turned out to span fifteen days. I prayed continually for God to bless us. In prayer, I lifted up my family to receive His protection and comfort. As the prosecution presented its case against Lacey, I was able to see fissures in the evidence, and I continued to believe God would answer my prayers.

chapter 24

Nanc's house was quiet when I awoke, and I was surprised that I had slept soundly. Maybe it was because the active portion of the trial was over and the jury wouldn't begin deliberations for a few more hours. Would the jurors decide Lacey's fate quickly? Would they drag it into the following day? Would we be celebrating? Or not?

I slipped out of bed—gently, trying not to disturb Ron. Nanc had set the timer on the coffee maker the night before, and the comforting aroma greeted me as I entered the empty kitchen. I filled a mug and wrapped my palms around it for warmth.

Ron entered the kitchen and poured himself a cup.

"Sleep well?" I asked.

"Not really." He took a long swallow.

Instead of making small talk, we looked out the bay windows to the far-away Enchantment Mountains. A sliver of morning sun shone through the clouds, then disappeared. In companionable silence, we sat at the table like this was any ordinary day. I didn't ask what he thought the jury would decide, or how long he thought it would take.

Al joined us, then Nanc. We finished off the pot of coffee. While Nanc made a fresh batch, Al prepared oatmeal, and

I put bread in the toaster. It was the same routine we had completed each morning of the trial—except today was different. Our bubble would be driving here to wait with us for the verdict.

Dena and Steve arrived around 10:00 a.m. I felt a fullness in my heart knowing that they were here early. Elaine and Sherise entered next, with muffins and fruit. As our gathering of friends grew, I felt strengthened by their loving presence. Conversations were conducted in hushed tones, as if we were outside an emergency room waiting for the announcement of life or death. Would we have a verdict today? I felt that the longer it took for the jury to decide, the better the outcome would be.

Danny and the kids had spent the night with Lacey in the trailer. Blaine and Meri bounded into the house to say good-bye. Lacey wanted them home before the verdict in case it didn't turn out well. Ron and I took turns hugging our grandchildren, and they also gave hugs to Al and Nanc and the rest of our friends. Such sweet kids. From their body language, I could tell that Lacey had kept her good-byes light. Nanc offered them a cookie on their way out the door. They smiled and waved as they climbed into Danny's truck. My heart clenched as I watched Lacey reach through the open window and touch their faces. I joined her on the gravel driveway, my arm tight around her shoulder. We waved until they were out of sight.

"We're going to get a good decision today, right, Mom?"

"I certainly hope so, sweetie."

✳ ✳ ✳

We received the call from the court a bit after 1:00 p.m. The jury had reached a verdict. It had only taken them four hours;

three if you deducted an hour for lunch. This could not be good. But maybe it was. Maybe they had all agreed quickly that Lacey was innocent.

Ron, Lacey, and I, along with our bubble, drove to the courthouse. When we entered the courtroom and all eyes turned our way, I felt like we were on stage.

Lacey joined Haney and Tad at the defense table. We took our seats as we had each day of trial. Our friends surrounded us.

"All rise."

The guilty verdict had been declared. Ron folded Lacey into his protective bear hug. The agony on his face caused me to flee out the courtroom doors, down three flights of stairs, and collapse bawling in the isolated employees' courtyard. Some of our friends came to look for me, the other half for Ron where he had taken sanctuary in a dark hallway. They found him with his forehead against the wall, sobbing into the elbow of his coat. Al stayed with him.

Our friends gathered Ron and me in time to watch the deputies whisk Lacey down the first-floor hallway. In their dark uniforms, they looked like foreboding bookends with Lacey in handcuffs between them. At least this time, she didn't have the belly chain and shackles. This time, her hands were simply cuffed behind her back.

Her eyes were cast downward. A gasp escaped my mouth as I saw her defeated posture. Ron came to my side. Our group fell in line behind us as we followed Lacey out the front courthouse doors. The squad car was parked close to the exit. Matt stood near the open rear door. I'd never seen the backseat of a patrol car or the indented seat crevice designed to accommodate the handcuffs. My claustrophobic fear of being restrained rose like bile in my throat.

Stepping toward Matt, tears streaming down my face, I said, "Matt, at least let her have her hands in front of her; she gets carsick."

Ron gently drew me backward. The deputies maneuvered Lacey into the backseat. Her head remained in a hangdog position; she showed no awareness that we were near. Our friends huddled around us as the squad car drove away. I remember shivering, but it wasn't from the cold.

Dena wanted to drive us home. I told her we were okay, but Ron gave her the car keys anyway. In my quick exit from the courtroom, I hadn't witnessed his breakdown. I was so shaken by my unanswered prayers that I wasn't aware how much my husband was also hurting. He sat in the passenger seat. I bunched our coats and myself on the backseat, along with my purse and Lacey's. When she had handed it to me, she had pointed to an envelope inside.

Pawing through her purse now, I said, "Hon, Lacey left something for us." Opening the envelope, I unfolded the paper and began to read it aloud:

"If you are reading this, then the verdict did not go our way. I love you Dad and Mom, and I am thankful for all you have done for me. I'm sorry it's come to this. Here is a scripture that I find helpful . . ."

Ron covered his face with his hands as I continued reading Lacey's words.

"2 Timothy 4:7-8. I have fought the good fight. . . ."

"Bonnie. Stop," Ron pleaded as he torqued his head against the headrest like a whiplash victim. Tears escaped his closed eyes and settled upon his lashes.

I scooted back in the seat and read the rest of Lacey's letter to myself. Then I began silently rehashing the evidence, the testimony, the prosecution's statements, and our lawyer's defense. I tried to assimilate the reason for the guilty verdict.

Why this outcome, God? Dena's husband, Steve, followed us in their car. Ron would take over driving when we reached our restaurant, and they would continue to their home.

It was dusk when Ron drove us past our house and out to Lacey's. We wanted to make sure that Danny had heard the verdict and that Blaine and Meri were okay.

The apple trees along the way were barren of leaves. The river looked like a vast, dark ribbon. As we neared her place, flames soared above the treetops surrounding Lacey's doublewide. Had Danny set the house ablaze? Was he high on meth? Where were Blaine and Meri? Hastening our arrival down the pitted lane, we saw that the raging fire was in the middle of the lawn. It illuminated the evening sky. Danny was frantically throwing more brush and lumber scraps onto it. The flames spiked higher.

Meri ran to me as I got out of the car. I hoisted her up. Her skinny legs wrapped around my waist as I swayed side to side and cooed into her ear, "Shhh, sweetie, shhh."

She kept sobbing, "I want my mommy. I want my mommy."

Blaine's tear-filled eyes reflected the flares of the fire. Ron gathered him and held his trembling body close. The four of us watched a possessed Danny throw more wood onto the fire.

"Lacey was cold the last time she was in jail," Danny hollered. "I promised her if she ever had to be there again, I'd build her a gigantic fire."

Oddly, that made sense. That single sentence said he knew the outcome of the verdict and that Lacey was back in the same jail as when she was first arrested. At once the blazing fire, which had appeared menacing when we first saw it, took on an almost comforting presence. Danny stepped closer to Ron and Blaine. All three stared, trance-like, into the dancing flames.

I moved closer to the glow, trying to keep Meri warm.

Her stranglehold loosened when Danny's mom and brother arrived. They planned to stay the night with Danny and the kids and possibly extend their stay through the next few days. By the time Ron and I left, our grandkids were calmer. We gave Blaine Lacey's cell phone so he could call if he needed us.

Our next stop was Trilby's. She'd also heard the verdict. In this new world of Facebook, everyone had known the outcome before we left the courthouse. We comforted her the best we could and struggled to answer the question we had asked ourselves all along: *How did it all go so wrong?*

Leaving Trilby's, I felt like I was underwater in the deep end of a pool, my lungs deprived of oxygen, without the willpower to try to surface.

chapter 25

When we arrived home to our darkened house, Ron turned on the overhead kitchen light, and we both went straight to our recliners. The light filtering in from the kitchen cast shadows over us.

Numb from the shock of the day's events, we sat silent for quite a while before Ron asked, "Bonnie, who do you need to have with you, to give you comfort? I'll call them tomorrow for you."

At first, it slayed me that he thought I needed anyone but him to help me get through Lacey's conviction. Then I realized his offer was made from genuine love for me. He understood we would be incapable of bolstering each other. I think I loved him more at that moment than at any other time in our marriage.

"Hon, I don't know. I don't know what I need." Tears cascaded down my cheeks. I pulled a wadded Kleenex from my pocket and blotted the salty flow until the tissue was soaked. My tears continued to fall. "I don't know anything anymore." Sobbing out loud, I could hardly breathe. I looked toward Ron, but in the darkness his features were unreadable. "Who can I get for you? To comfort you?"

"I don't know. Part of me just wants to run off to the cabin and get drunk, but I want you with me, and I know you'll want to stay close to Blaine and Meri."

Thinking about Lacey's kids and what this guilty verdict would do to their young lives, my tears increased and fell unrestrained down my face. "Yeah," I said, "I'll need to stay near." My body felt drained of life.

I don't believe I slept at all that night. My mind still churned out questions as if it had yet to realize the trial was over. There was no need to continue examining every detail, every motive, every reaction, and every comment. Our daughter had been convicted of murder. She was in the county jail, waiting to be processed to go to prison.

Instead of tossing and turning and allowing my mind to continue to spin, I got up and wrote in my journal:

> *I feel like I've been hit between the eyes with a 2x4. I used to think I had a good feel of what was going to happen and that my faith would work miracles. I don't know what to think now. I'm not angry, I'm confused. In my logical mind, I need to make sense of this. Please, Lord, be with me as I travel this next journey. I lift my family to You and pray You can keep them safe and protected. I don't know Your plans, Lord, and I am torn apart because I feel You failed Lacey and me. Please give her strength and peace of heart. Help her find other inmates who believe in God and please protect her.*
>
> *Lord, give me insight so I may understand Your plan. Keep me from becoming bitter. Help me to not crawl into my shell. Lead me to be more perceptive to those around*

*me and guide me to know what to do to help Blaine and
Meri as they adjust to life without their mother. Protect
them and help them to also know Your goodness.*

Reading that journal entry years later, I realized God
must have been in my heart as I wrote it. I don't recognize
the woman who could have written those words so soon after
her daughter was convicted. But it's my handwriting. And I
remember writing in my journal early that morning when sleep
eluded me. How could I have sounded that calm?

I also wrote a note to those who hadn't been with us in
court. The time stamp on the email was 4:42 a.m.

Dear Friends and Family,
*Our hearts are heavy. The jury came back with a guilty
verdict at 2:16 p.m. yesterday. We are trying to make
sense of it and know it will take us some time to realize
the totality of life in prison without parole. I would
appreciate any scripture or inspirational verses that
you would care to share to help me keep my faith and
remain strong. Thank you all for traveling this road
with us. Lacey left Ron and me a thank you note with
this scripture.*

*2 Timothy 4:7–8. I have fought the good fight, I have
finished the race, I have kept the faith.*

Love, Bonnie

Reaching for my Woman's Devotional Bible, I held it vertically
between my palms and allowed the pages to open randomly.

Nothing it revealed gave me comfort. Emotionally shattered, I felt forgotten by God. Did He not hear my prayers? Was I not devout enough? Did I not pray correctly? How could this be part of His plan? Did He not hear Lacey's prayers either? How can this be the highest good?

Tears slid down my face and created wet spots on the parchment pages of the Bible. I had never questioned my faith; it had always stood beside me, guaranteeing me a good life. I had believed if I prayed hard enough, beseeched God for His protection of my daughter, that we would all come out of this unscathed. I had entertained the idea that possibly her arrest *had* been for her protection—not the way Matt had meant, but maybe there had been a hit out on her the night she was arrested, and God had stepped in and put her in jail to keep her safe. Now I told myself that maybe He had a better plan for her than anything I could imagine. My mind clamored for reasons to believe that He had not forsaken my daughter or me.

HIRST-PAVEK GUILTY OF ALL CHARGES
The jury in the murder trial of Lacey Hirst-Pavek reached a guilty verdict just after 2 p.m. on Tuesday, after beginning deliberations at 9 a.m. Hirst-Pavek was on trial for her involvement in the murder of Selena Clark during the early morning hours of March 1, 2009. Judge Jim Barlow announced the jury's guilty verdict for Hirst-Pavek's charges of first-degree premeditated murder and first-degree manslaughter of an unborn quick child. Hirst-Pavek's parents and assorted family members were in the courtroom when she was declared guilty of all charges, including the aggravated circumstances of an accomplice using a

*deadly weapon and knowing the victim was pregnant
before the crime was committed.*

Why had God withheld His grace in our situation? Why
had He let me down? How could I continue to pray and believe
in His goodness now?

I knew I shouldn't doubt Him, but I was bereft.

Where is He now?

chapter 26

On our first visit to see Lacey in jail, we met up with Danny, Blaine, and Meri in the parking lot. Snow stuck to the sidewalk, except where the ice-melt pellets crunched under our feet. Entering the same waiting room where Ron and I had bailed Lacey out felt like déjà vu . . . except this time our daughter would not be exiting the buzzing door.

The elevated office that watched over the waiting room also gave visual access to the visiting areas. Only three visitors were allowed to visit at one time, so Danny escorted the kids to Lacey's cubicle as Ron and I waited our turn. I felt the same as I had that day a year and a half before: diminished, and in great need of pity. I worried about Blaine and Meri and what it would do to their spirits seeing their mom behind the glass and not being able to touch her. I feared that the trauma of her arrest and subsequent imprisonment would create carnage in their young lives.

Danny and the kids visited for twenty minutes, then rejoined Ron and me. Meri clung to Danny's arm and sobbed into his shirt. Blaine stood apart, a shell-shocked look on his face.

I struggled between wanting to stay and help console them and my need to see Lacey. My desire to see my daughter won. After kissing each grandchild on the top of the head, I walked down the narrow hallway with Ron and entered the visiting stall.

It was like you see in the movies: heavy Plexiglas separated you from the prisoner. An old-fashioned black telephone receiver hung on the wall to speak to your loved one through. There was one seat: a flat, circular piece of wood bolted to a steel post. Lacey was already seated on her side of the divider. Her eyes were puffy and red from crying. Seeing us, she picked up her phone mouthpiece and motioned for us to do the same.

The static in the earpiece and the low volume of Lacey's voice made it difficult to hear her through the receiver. I watched her lips move, but I couldn't understand what she was saying. It was like she was a million miles away instead of mere inches. Ron guided me to sit on the stool, and as I put my hand to the glass, Lacey mirrored my outstretched palm. I mouthed *I love you*, then gave the receiver to Ron.

We didn't stay long. Visiting time was limited, and we cut our visit short so Danny and the kids could see her again.

⁕⁕⁕⁕

I wrote her a letter when we arrived home.

> *Lacey,*
> *We have just come from visiting you in jail. As I sit here in my home office, the snow is swirling in lofty flakes outside my window. It is collecting in drifts on the stairs, and then a gust of wind comes by and changes the pile. That is how I have felt thru this new journey we are on. My tears are like the snow; they swirl at times in my eyes but do not fall. At other times, they fall freely down my face, and I sob until I am unable*

to breathe. I love you so much and hate that you have to endure this. Then I feel guilty for crying; you are the one who is suffering this injustice in the first person. I can only imagine your days. Remember the rainbow on the first day of court? I believe God is still with us and those colors were His promise to us that He would never forsake us. We don't know what His plan is—and this part of it sucks—but I know if we continue to trust in Him, He will protect you. You are an amazing woman, kiddo. I am proud that you are my daughter.
Love, Mom

I felt like a fraud. I kept telling Lacey that everything would be okay, but behind the scenes, I questioned my faith in God. He had let me down. It seemed that my entire life of praying and believing that He would bring about the highest good was a sham. God had not answered my prayers for Lacey's protection. I dove into the pity pit at home. I felt as if the walls were closing in on me. I still appeared to be functioning, but on the inside, I was a wreck. I was back to not knowing how to ask for help. I didn't know what kind of help I needed.

I had a full-blown breakdown in the shower, my preferred crying place. Wailing at the top of my lungs, my anguish sounded like a walrus call. I allowed the hot water to pelt my skin until it felt like a sandblaster had annihilated it. I turned the temperature to cool, to temper the pain.

Toweling off, I noticed a cobweb in the furthest corner of the ceiling. The light from the window reflected on the tiny strands. I watched as a hairy spider approached a fly and began spinning its sticky strings around it. The translucent web moved in rhythm with the spider. The faint buzzing of the fly's wings stopped when the entanglement was complete. My mind likened that fly to Lacey: she was now trapped, helpless, inside the deceitful web of the justice system.

One of the legalities of being sent to prison includes giving up the custody of your children. Tad prepared the custody papers in which Ron and I, along with Danny, were the petitioners and Lacey was the respondent. The Findings of Fact and Conclusions of Law in the Nonparental Custody papers gave us and Danny fifty-fifty joint custody of Blaine and Meri.

To the court system, this was just another detail that needed to be completed before Lacey could be moved to prison. She was now a possession of the state and had no rights. For me, it felt like a giant hammer was pounding a square peg into the round hole of my heart. Usurping Lacey's rights to her own children felt reprehensible. I was consumed with worry and motherly guilt. I felt I hadn't been outspoken enough, or wise enough, or aware enough to have stopped bad things from happening to my family.

chapter 27

Lacey's sentencing day was purely a formality since the judge had no choice but to render life without parole. The 1981 Sentencing Reform Act of Washington State granted little variance in sentencing timelines. I had imagined Lacey arriving at court in socked feet; a drug-sniffing dog had yet to be brought in to clear her tennis shoes. I dreamt she would be shackled and handcuffed to a short chain that would force her to bend low and hobble unevenly into the courtroom.

My relief when I saw her in shoes and without shackles seemed foolish when I remembered the severity of the sentence to be brought down on her that day.

Our eyes connected briefly as she scanned the room for friendly faces—or, possibly, looked to see if Danny was there. His presence would have provoked outrage from Selena's family. He had stayed home that day with the kids, where he should have been all along; without his infidelity, or the drugs, neither we nor Selena's family would have suffered our traumatic losses.

Lacey was clad in a dark red, jail-issued jumpsuit. A deputy escorted her to the table where Haney and Tad were seated.

Our bubble had joined us for this final court date. They brought me comfort in the hostile courtroom, which was filled with Selena's family and friends. I prayed for calm in my heart, to be able to endure this final step without breaking down in tears. Selena's mom and sister each addressed the court, sharing how Selena's death had affected them. As I listened to their pain-filled words, I sent up prayers for comfort and healing for them.

Lacey's appeal was filed before we left the courtroom that day. It gave me hope. I wanted to believe that God was still watching over my family. I was encouraged that there could be a tiny ray of light at the end of this very dark tunnel. With an appeal, surely God could work his wonders, and positive things could still come out of this.

Shopping for groceries later that week, I had a wistful smile on my face, imagining Lacey winning her appeal, when I felt a tap on my shoulder. When I turned, a longtime friend stood before me, her eyes glistening with unshed tears. She gave me a fervent hug and whispered in my ear, "I'm so sorry for you and your family."

Her raw emotion brought me back to reality.

"Thank you," I squeaked.

She was the type to genuinely feel the pain of a friend. She didn't want a conversation, only to let me know she cared. We both swiped at our tears, nodded acknowledgment, turned, and continued our shopping. I was overcome with love, sadness, and then shame in myself for my analytical thinking. Earlier, I had compartmentalized our situation. The trial was over:

check mark. Sentencing was over: check mark. Lacey's appeal had been filed: check mark. I'd been telling myself we would move on to the next hurdle with hope.

But how could I have hope or even choose to smile when my daughter had been convicted of murder and sentenced to life in prison?

I looked at my long shopping list, only partially completed, and headed to the dairy case for eggs. My optimism tumbled back into self-doubt and recrimination. I was unable to keep up the façade. I wiped away spilling tears and was unable to continue shopping.

In the checkout lane, I kept my eyes and face downcast. *Please, Lord, don't let me see anyone else I know.* Next to the cash register was the weekly paper with Lacey's mug shot: *WIFE SENTENCED TO LIFE WITHOUT PAROLE.*

Should I buy the newspaper so I could read what twists and untruths were printed? Or should I pretend it didn't matter what everyone else believed? I chose the latter, even though my moist, red eyes told a different story.

chapter 28

Thanksgiving was the week of Lacey's sentencing, and the entire family gathered at our house. Lacey wrote a message for me to read in lieu of my usual grace:

> *Although I can make a long list of things I am NOT thankful for, I would like everyone to know that I am very thankful for the family that sits in this kitchen today. I am thankful that my children are loved and fed. There are many in the world that are not. I am thankful for the bond that each of you has created in this most difficult time. I love you all . . . now stop crying and eat!*
> *Love, Lacey*
> *P.S. Eat a plate for me too and know that I am not alone today . . . for I have the love of my family and God.*

What incredible strength and grace God must have given Lacey for her to share that with us. If she was able to be thankful even after the verdict, I thought, I needed to reconsider my thinking. I gathered the bundle of cards we had received when

Lacey was first arrested, and set about sending out thank-you notes in return.

Each time I started to write, my scrawl presented itself toddler-like across the page. My handwriting on a good day is barely legible, so I'm not sure what I had been thinking, but I felt it was important to send a personalized thank-you to each well-wisher to show our appreciation. I cried as I reread each card. We were truly blessed with good friends.

I finally succumbed to printing from my computer instead:

We give thanks for friends like you. Your thoughtful note warmed our hearts. Your kind gesture will last a lifetime. Thank you! Love, Ron and Bonnie

I also created thank-you cards for our bubble, with individual sentiments for each person. My creations fell short in the design phase, but I hoped the magnitude of love and appreciation Ron and I had for each of them would shine through. Their willingness to help us through the court proceedings had been a heavenly gift.

———————

Lacey was still in the county jail, waiting to be transferred to the women's prison three hundred miles away. She provided me with the information to begin the paperwork for us to visit her after she was shipped out. The Department of Corrections Visitor's Questionnaire wanted each visitor's social security number and driver's license information, plus answers to the following questions:

- Have you ever been involved in illegal or criminal activity with the offender?

- Are you presently under active supervision by any state or local criminal justice entity?
- Have you ever been convicted of a felony?
- Are you a US citizen?

I received a thick booklet in return, the *DOC Guide for Family and Friends of Incarcerated Offenders*. Lacey would not be referred to as a prisoner in prison; she would soon become an Incarcerated Offender in a Corrections Center. Maximum security, her designated home for the first four years, was instead named Close Custody Unit (CCU). Nowhere in the booklet was the word "cell"; her living quarters were described as her "room." I questioned how this new terminology came into place. No matter how they sugarcoated the words, Lacey would soon be a prisoner in a maximum-security prison and would be relegated to a cell.

On the last day of November, we received a call from the local jail that our contact visit with Lacey had been granted and scheduled for that day. Danny, Blaine, Meri, Ron, Trilby, Rylee, and I all crowded into a tiny, locked room with Lacey. Danny reacted to the confined space as if he were the one imprisoned. Sweated poured from him, his hands fidgeted, and he shot paranoid looks at the observation window above us. After he hugged and kissed Lacey, he migrated to the outer edges of the room, I concentrated on sending love to Lacey and tried to not be angry with Danny about his behavior. This would be our last time with her for several months. I wanted to absorb every minute allocated to us.

Holding Lacey so we were heart to heart, I told her, "You are a good person, sweetie. Don't ever doubt that." Blaine snuggled in close. Meri cuddled into the front of her. Lacey's anxiousness calmed as she wrapped her arms around her children. Trilby massaged Lacey's neck. Ron gathered everyone close. Tears flowed freely. Tears of loss. Tears of pain. Tears of fear of the unknown.

⚹

When our visit ended, we said sorrow-filled good-byes and stepped outside. The crisp winter air was refreshing after all that time in the stuffy room. Fresh snow covered the ground. Lacey wouldn't be able to experience snow in prison, as it rarely snowed on the western side of the state. We gathered outside the jail, under the rusty, barred window we hoped she was watching from. It didn't seem right to leave her there alone. Blaine and Meri didn't want to go until they saw their mom in the window. Finally, someone tapped on a pane above us and we waved toward the sound.

"Hey kids," I coaxed, "let's make your mom a snow angel."

Meri was the first to plop backward into the fluffy whiteness and sweep her arms and legs in unison, making angel impressions. Blaine followed suit, along with Trilby, Rylee, and me. It felt glorious making angels for Lacey. Outlines in the snow that would show her our love. It also felt like a bit of defiance, leaving our imprints on the jail grounds.

I found out later that Lacey wasn't the one who had tapped on the window. She never saw the snow angels we created.

chapter 29

Lacey was shipped to prison via the DOC chain (Department of Corrections transport) the day after our snow angels. She was allowed to keep her Bible until she was transferred to the next van that would take her to the women's prison.

I was heartsick when I received the call from the local jail to come and pick up her Bible. She must have felt entirely pulverized losing her beautiful scriptures. I was fully intending to go the following day to retrieve it—until I pictured myself breaking down into a blathering mess, at which point I asked Ron if he would go. I wrote a thank-you note to the jail staff— Lacey said they had been kind to her—and Ron delivered the card when he picked up her belongings.

＊ ＊ ＊ ＊ ＊

Opening the Bible that had been taken from Lacey, I scanned the scriptures she had highlighted and realized her English Standard Version and my New International Version read quite differently.

"I think I'll order myself a Bible of the same version as Lacey," I told Ron, "so that when she shares scripture, I get the same meaning."

I could have used Lacey's Bible, but that seemed sacrilegious. Her red leather holy book was intimate to her, and I wouldn't feel right marking or notating verses on her pages.

"You might order some for Blaine, Meri, Danny, and Trilby too," Ron said, "so they can follow along when she shares with them."

I purchased hand-sized Bibles for all of us, and had each person's name engraved in golden script on the covers. Lacey supplied scriptures for each person from the Bible I had ordered for her from Christianbooks.com. I highlighted the lines and marked each page with a tiny yellow sticky tab. I proposed to Lacey that these could be Christmas presents from her. She loved the idea and wrote notes for each one; I taped them neatly into the front covers. Wrapping them with extra care, I chose hot pink paper for Meri, dark red for Blaine, blue for Danny, and teal for Trilby. I topped each with a resplendent bow.

Neither Blaine nor Meri were very impressed with receiving a Bible for a present. They were still at the age that money or Xbox games were the gold standard.

The note Lacey wrote for mine said;

To my wonderful and beautiful mother,
Words can't express the love and appreciation I have for
you, Mom. You are the glue that holds this chaos we call
family together. You are a true matriarch. We have to
continue to believe that there is a purpose for this road
we are on. We have to believe that someday we will
look back together and see the lesson or meaning of all
of it. We have to believe that God doesn't want me here
forever—but is testing all of our faiths and weaknesses

*and our strength and love. I love you, Mom. You are
the best friend a girl could hope to have, and I hope
my daughter feels the same way someday even with the
distance that separates us now. Love, Lacey*

My heart overflowed with her words. The trust she placed
in God was a blessing to me, and I thanked Him often for
coming into her life. I believe her heavenly devotion was the
key that kept me functioning—the strength that kept me
believing that His highest good would still be found.

The jail chaplain told Lacey that the path she had just traveled
had been predetermined before she was born. I understand his
meaning: God has a plan for each of us. But I don't whole-
heartedly agree that it is set in stone. I believe our destiny is
molded by the choices we make along the way. The goodness
we show people and the kindness we share with others—aren't
those what are important in a godly world?

I searched my Bible for understanding. Why this path
for my family? I found comfort in some passages, but others
portrayed a vengeful God. The God I believed in had always
brought me comfort and peace and strength to get through the
difficult times. Was this a test of my faith? What connection
did our current journey have with God's overall plan? Were
we but pawns in a more significant story?

Everything and everyone had changed, especially me. I mentioned to Ron that I didn't know who I was anymore, and his
reply fractured me: "Bonnie, don't you think I feel the same way?"

I was unable to respond. We stood toe to toe, but the distance between us felt more like that between the goalposts of a football field. Our eyes dimmed and our expressions slackened downward as the weight of our despair became too much to share. Instead of reaching toward each other, we retreated. Tears cascaded down my face as I walked to our bedroom. I heard Ron go outside.

How were we to move forward now that Lacey was in prison? Why hadn't God protected her? My misery consumed me. I crawled into my protective shell like a turtle pulls its head and legs in tight when it's in danger. I secured imaginary blinders around my vision, believing that if I muted my awareness of the world, I wouldn't feel as much pain. I avoided people who might offer sympathy or compassion. Life felt somewhat saner with blinders on.

———✳———✳———✳———

After gassing up my car at the two-pump station, I entered the quaint store to pay. When I glanced at the neatly stacked newspapers by the front door, I didn't expect to see Lacey on the front page: it was the first of January, and she had been locked away in prison for over a month. So my heart plunged when I saw a picture of her being handcuffed in the courtroom. Her hands were behind her back, and her Sherpa coat gaped open as a deputy concentrated on securing her restraints. Tad was in the background, his arms crossed over his ribcage.

The sadness on Lacey's face in the photo—the way her chin was crinkled from trying not to cry—torched me with motherly pain. I hadn't seen this picture before. I always thought her mug shot was horrendous, but this one impaled my soul.

TOP STORIES IN 2010: MURDER, THE ECONOMY

Four convictions in Selena Clark's death, head the list. (The caption under her picture) Okanogan County Sheriff's Sgt. handcuffs Lacey Kae Hirst-Pavek after her November conviction in the murder of Selena Clark.

chapter 30

We drove over the second of two snowy mountain passes; Ron and I were escorting Blaine and Meri to the prison to visit their mom. I agonized over what the day would produce. Would our visit be in a small cubicle and through glass, as it had been at the county jail? Would the phones be of better quality? How many of us would fit in the room at a time? What would Lacey's state of mind be?

When I wrote to her, I pretended she was just down the street, or away at school. Now, actually seeing her in prison, I would not be allowed that deception.

We arrived on time, even with a multitude of traffic delays on I-5. The west side of the state buzzed with freeways—so different from our rural county, which boasted only one stoplight. I had asked God for safe and timely travels, and He'd delivered us through the maze of concrete overpasses and exit ramps.

Tall chain-link fences topped with curled wire verified we were in the right place.

Clutching our clearance papers, we checked in at the front desk. The guard's actions were precise as he examined our IDs and took a picture of each of us for the DOC visiting records.

We were assigned a table number for our visit, and a key to a locker where we were instructed to leave our belongings.

We proceeded to the next station, where we removed our shoes and passed through a metal detector like we would at an airport. When cleared, our hands were stamped with invisible ink, and we joined other visitors waiting at a third barricade. We stood there until our group began to overflow, at which point the guards guided us outside to the next blockade. Between buildings, a gentle mist of rain fell. We gathered at a steel gate. It buzzed open.

We moved like cattle into an enclosure. The gate we passed through clanged shut before we were allowed passage to the next station. Razor wire coiled like a giant Slinky on the ground and double-ringed the top of the fence that surrounded us. The shiny barbs overwhelmed me. I felt like we were being imprisoned also. A panicked desire to turn around and leave swelled in my body, but the doors behind us were shut. There was no escape.

As the multitude of visitors around us wedged into the small interior room, Ron and I sheltered Blaine and Meri between us. The guards in their raised station behind tinted glass waited for the door behind us to close and then triggered a massive steel door in front of us to slide mechanically open. Everyone formed another line, and each family gave the guard their inmate's name.

Our assigned table had the number carved deeply into the top of it, similar to the old-time school desks that had a deep groove for pencils. The room was the total opposite of what I had expected. It was wide open, like a cafeteria. There were thirty-seven tables.

The room filled with visitors seeking their table number. The inmates arrived and formed a line to check in at the guard desk. Meri spotted her mom and cried, "There she is!"

Lacey smiled and gave us a slight wave of greeting. We watched other visitors as their inmates joined them. Protocol seemed to be to stay at the table until Lacey joined us. We nodded and waited. Her five-foot-four frame appeared thinner. Her short hair was growing out. She wore gray sweatpants and a gray T-shirt.

When she made it to the table, Blaine and Meri burrowed close to her side. Ron and I gathered them all into a group hug and then watched other visitors line up at various vending machines. Lacey wanted a Dr. Pepper, so Blaine and I loaded our arms with enough goodies, sandwiches, and Peanut M&M's, to sustain us for the three-hour visit. I was glad I had read the entire visitors pamphlet (multiple times) and knew to purchase the prepaid vending card. No cash was allowed in the visiting area.

The room took on a welcoming aura, blended conversations permeating the space as families reunited. I considered our own table, and I sent up thanks that Lacey was okay and we were able to be with her. Meri wanted to play Yahtzee, so over the din of the rattling dice, our little group spent the time chit-chatting and snacking on munchies. With the addition of the M&M's, it almost felt like we were back at my kitchen table.

The allotted time whizzed by. I was stunned when the guard at the raised station announced that visiting was over. We hugged Lacey and joined the other visitors in the exit line. As we filed out, our daughter sat with the other inmates, all in their matching gray shirts and sweatpants. They would be searched before they returned to their cells.

The heavy steel door opened. We crowded into the tight enclosure. The portal behind us slid closed. The exit in front of us buzzed open, and as we walked toward the compound with the offensive razor wire, Meri began to cry. I wrapped my arm around her, and our tears joined. It felt unseemly, leaving

Lacey there. Blaine walked close to Ron, and Ron's muscular arm snagged him in tight. Our group was silent as we passed through each buzzing, clanging gate.

When we arrived at the front lobby, we swept our stamped hands under a black light. The invisible marker magically appeared. We were cleared to leave.

chapter 31

National reporters never showed up on our doorstep, but the *National Enquirer* ran a nasty story about Lacey. The tabloid's front page brandished a close-up of Kirstie Alley with the buttons of her shirt straining against rolls of flesh. Scandal readers would have been the only ones to see page forty, but the local paper headlined it also:

MURDER STORY MAKES TABLOID: EVIL WIFE PUTS HIT ON HUBBY'S MISTRESS
Hired killers brutally stab pregnant girlfriend

I was in the checkout lane at Safeway when I saw the headline with Lacey's picture—the gut-searing one of her being handcuffed—along with a photo of the *Enquirer*'s front page. Pain burned through me like salt rubbed into a gaping wound. Would it never end? Lacey was in prison. The case was over. We had lost. How many more times would I come face to face with my daughter's picture on the front page? It was incidents like this that tossed me back into hiding and questioning God.

What's next, Lord? What more do we have to endure?

I wrote to Lacey every day, in the beginning—snail mail style. When prison email became available, I switched over to that. It was quicker, but my notes began to lose their sensitivity. I was attempting to keep my devastation from erupting in my writing by building a blockade around my heart. My emails became more about what her kids were doing and less about sharing my heart on the page. I became Lacey's secretary, and my correspondence dropped back to every other day. Until she asked too much from me, that is—like helping Danny navigate bill paying, or checking on him to make sure he was okay—and then I'd not write for many days because I knew my outrage would blaze my sentences with anger. Danny, I thought, should not be my responsibility. He should be able to accomplish things on his own. But since Blaine and Meri still lived with him, our lives continued to intertwine.

I prayed for guidance and grace to navigate the roles now cast upon me, although I wasn't always a willing participant. I took care of Lacey the best way I knew how: by becoming her lens into life outside prison walls. I detailed Blaine and Meri's itinerary for each week so she could visualize what they were doing at any given time. I think if our places were reversed, I'd have been so despondent I wouldn't even have wanted communication with the world I no longer had access to. Reminders of events I was missing would have been too painful for me. Lacey, however, was the opposite. She wanted to know everything.

Danny wrote Lacey many letters that she cherishes. In the first six months, he tried his darnedest to take care of Blaine and Meri. He took them to visit Lacey on her birthday, Valentine's Day, Easter, and Mother's Day. His devotion to her seemed to be what kept him going. He and I even attended a day-long event in the prison chapel with Lacey.

In that chapel setting, I witnessed the love between Danny and Lacey and marveled at how that was possible. How does a wife forgive a husband for cheating on her, let alone initiating a slew of events that landed her in prison? Would I ever be able to forgive Danny? He had wronged my daughter, and the only reason I was attending this event with him was because Lacey—knowing that I would be the facilitator who filled out the paperwork, drove the car, and arrived on time—had asked me to.

In the chapel, we sang my mom's favorite hymn, "I Come to the Garden Alone." Tears brimmed in my eyes but never fell. The words to the chorus reminded me that God walks with me, and He talks with me, and He tells me I am His own. I felt God's love surround us in the chapel that day, and I acknowledged that song as a sign that Mom's angelic wings were watching over Lacey too.

On our drive home, Danny said, "Thank you, Bonnie, for doing this. It meant a lot."

"You're welcome, Danny," I said. "It was good to see her happy." That was the most warmth I could muster.

Danny then closed his eyes and slept. That made the trip home more comfortable for both of us.

chapter 32

Blaine and Meri came to live with us eight months after Lacey went to prison. Danny had plummeted into depression and was unable to function, let alone be there emotionally for them. I wondered if I were any more capable. I've read stories of well-adjusted kids who were raised by their grandparents. I prayed this would be true for my grandchildren also.

It was the end of summer break when I went to the school to update Blaine and Meri's emergency contact information. Blaine was entering high school, and Meri middle school. Standing at the office counter, I updated their health insurance information, paid for lunch tickets, and changed their mailing address to ours. Scratching out Lacey and Danny's names, I entered Ron's and mine. The secretary looked at the crossed-out names and informed me that I needed to present legal forms to show that Ron and I were their guardians.

As I was driving home to get the paperwork, the magnitude of our situation slammed me. It was preposterous that I needed to present official paperwork to people I had known all my adult life to prove I was responsible for decisions and emergencies concerning my own grandchildren.

Nevertheless, I returned with the document, which I handed to the secretary. I hadn't thought to put it into an envelope, and the boldface heading—"Superior Court of Washington"—pulled one's eyes to its title. The phone rang, and the secretary placed the decree face-up on the counter—a few feet from me, and visible to prying eyes—as she visited with the caller. I felt like my daughter's downfall was again being laid out for all to see. I should have snatched it back off the counter, but instead I started to cry and escaped to my car.

Dear Lord, keep me strong. Thank You for bringing Blaine and Meri to us. Guide me in protecting and nurturing them. Help us to be the example they need in their lives. Assist their teachers and their friends to be kind and understanding.

<hr/>

Blaine and Meri's phones vibrating with alerts became commonplace in our house. Texts came and went with questions. *Who did you get for homeroom? What will you wear the first day?* Our full house settled into a routine of morning showers and the grandkids wrestling over the bathroom mirror.

Ron and I embraced our role of parenting. We assured Blaine and Meri they were safe, and we would be available to them at any time. Danny eventually moved out of state; after that, he rarely had contact with them.

My parenting style leaned toward the protective mode for the first few years. I saw my grandkids as wounded souls—not only from the small-town scrutiny where everyone knew what had happened but also from physically losing the security of their mother. I wanted to help them heal through our tutelage. Pictures of them the summer they came to live with us showed gangly, undernourished bodies, crooked teeth, and dark hollows sunk deep beneath their eyes. I never wanted to see them look like that again.

In between relishing day-to-day moments with Blaine

and Meri, I was conscience-stricken that I could celebrate milestones in their lives that Lacey couldn't. First dates, braces on, braces off, contact lenses instead of glasses, driver's licenses, first cars, first resumes, and first jobs—even daily nuances, like study habits, books read, and movies watched—would forever be hazed in melancholy. I felt ineligible to enjoy my life because my daughter was in prison and apart from her family. My fleeting feel-good moments got mired in the mud; I felt like a participant in a tractor pull, straining against a lead weight that has stopped them in their tracks.

Would I be able to be the nurturer my grandkids needed? Would I be able to help them overcome this tragedy?

chapter 33

The fall after Lacey's conviction, my dad flew up from Phoenix to visit her. Meeting him at the SEA-TAC airport, I had a knot in my heart. The little girl in me worried how he would handle the razor wire, the clanging gates, and the sight of his oldest grandchild behind bars. I prayed that God would bless our time together.

Growing up, Dad was the see-all, judgmental parent—the one who, with a scouring of his eyes, sized people up and sorted them into neat little categories: out-of-work bum, loose morals, good-for-nothing teenager. But he also saw the goodness in the stand-up guy and the hard worker with excellent manners. What category would he put Lacey into now?

Greeting him at the baggage carousel, I underwent his usual scrutiny. Then I saw his countenance soften to concern and felt generosity in his hug. As we drove to the prison, he explained that after the initial shock, he had decided the most positive thing he could do for Lacey was to love her and support her in whatever way she needed. When I glanced at him in the passenger seat, I saw a seasoned man with a tender heart. He pulled his handkerchief and dabbed at his eyes. Blinking my tears away, I concentrated on the backed-up traffic and maneuvered to the correct exit ramp.

Dad was not known for his patience. I was anxious about what his reaction to the prison security and visiting protocol would be. I watched for his usual signs of deep inhales, loud exhales, thumb bobs against his trousers, and jaw clenching. What I witnessed instead was an elder ingesting all that surrounded him with empathy. He survived the waits and the razor wire, and when he saw Lacey waiting in line to check in with the guard station, his eyes filled with tears. He pulled his handkerchief from his pocket—I'm not sure how he got it through security, pockets are supposed to be emptied—and forcefully blew his nose, then tucked the hanky back into his pocket as Lacey approached. She seemed hesitant, but he drew her into the most prolonged hug I have ever witnessed from him. They were going to be okay. God had answered my prayer. Our three-hour visit whizzed by.

Over the years, Dad was Lacey's most regular letter writer. He would share Bible verses, send her money for postage, and renew her subscriptions for crossword puzzles so she could keep her mind sharp. He became a huge blessing for Lacey, and thus for me also.

chapter 34

When I was summoned to Superior Court for jury duty a year after Lacey's verdict, I was intrigued to see the courtroom from the juror's perspective. Would being a juror give me insight into how Lacey could have been convicted? Could a procedure in the jury room have been shortcut? Could one juror have prodded the others into a guilty verdict? I wondered how much power one juror could hold over the others. If I sat on a jury, might I learn something that could help in Lacey's appeal? I was grasping at straws, but I needed a way to make sense of her conviction.

Approaching the courthouse for the first time since Lacey's sentencing, unease and darkness fell upon me. Once I stepped inside, I felt enshrouded in a tomb. My mind battled with itself. *Just walk up to the clerk of court, Bonnie, and ask to be excused.* I didn't know if I could handle sitting in the same courtroom again. But a large part of me wanted to try. *Suck it up, Bonnie,* I told myself, *you can do this.*

My heart hammered in my chest as I passed through the metal detector and joined the other fifty prospective jurors on the benches. The clerk asked us to rise as the judge entered. Judge Cone. I hadn't thought this through very well. He was the judge who'd ruled against Lacey and Danny living together during her bail period. Lacey's saga came alive in my body. It felt like she was on trial again. Closing my eyes, I slowed my breathing and asked God to help me regain my composure.

Jury selection began. We were each assigned a paddle with a number so Judge Cone could identify us by number and not by name. In a big city that is probably a befitting procedure, but in our small county, it felt pointless: I knew more than half of the people who sat in the courtroom with me.

Basic questions first:

1. Do you speak and understand English?
2. Do you have any medical issues that would cause you distress if you served for a week?
3. Would serving for a week create a hardship for you?

Several people raised their paddles and explained their need to be excused from jury duty. I had yet to hold up my paddle. The judge introduced the prosecutor and the detective who would be presenting evidence. As they entered from the back of the room, my eyes connected with Matt, the detective. I was enraged to see he and the same prosecutor would present this case also. Just being in the same room with them, fury rushed through my veins. My heart assaulted my ribcage. My temples throbbed.

"If you know either of these two gentlemen," said Judge Cone, "please raise your paddle."

The judge's words and the room seemed hazed in unreality. My arm felt glued to my side, and my paddle remained down.

Judge Cone asked for specifics from those with raised paddles, excused two people who were related to them, and then asked his next question: "Would anyone find themselves prejudiced against the prosecutor or the lead detective?"

Slowly, my paddle rose. My desire to be chosen for jury duty and my need to exit the courtroom were at extreme odds. I wanted to shout for all to hear, *Yes, I would be prejudiced against them because I believe they would do anything to get a guilty verdict!* The artery on the side of my neck pulsated. My right eyelid spasmed.

Judge Cone called my number. "I wondered when you would raise your paddle. Why would you be prejudiced?"

My voice came out so falsetto that I didn't even recognize it. "The prosecutor tried my daughter's case." Tears rolled down my cheeks, and I wiped them away with a trembling hand.

"Why would that prejudice you?" he asked by rote—but before I could answer, he saw me wilting and said, "You are excused."

Through watery eyes, I gathered my purse and rushed to the exit. My anguish was too much to hold in. I'm sure everyone in the room heard my choked release. I bolted down the stairs, lurched out of the courthouse, and scurried to my car. My whole body was trembling. I couldn't get away quick enough. I retrieved my keys from my purse and dropped them on the pavement. When I reached for them, my head collided with the side mirror. Damn.

I was sobbing feverishly and could barely see to put the keys in the ignition. I edged my car out of the lot, steered one block down the street, and parked under a large maple tree.

Why, God? Why? I bawled until I was spent.

chapter 35

How do the soul, the heart, the mind know when to start healing? Is there a magic timeline? When my mom died in 1995, I grieved daily. Holidays were especially challenging: Christmas, her birthday in January, Easter, Mother's Day.

Back then, at our smaller restaurant on Mother's Day, we gave a rose to each mother who dined with us. In the pre-dawn hours, I snipped the sharp thorns and wrapped each stem in green plastic wrap. The sweet aroma from the buckets of flowers outpaced the morning smells of bacon and hash browns. I enjoyed presenting each delighted mother with a rose. But the year Mom died, each time I offered a "Happy Mother's Day," my heart wept. One woman so resembled her that I rushed to my office before my customers or employees could witness my meltdown.

On the anniversary of Mom's death, she came to me in dream state. I smelled her Dare perfume and felt her love encapsulate me as she whispered, *Bonnie, I am in a splendid place. You need to heal now.* I woke up with peace in my soul and knew that her spirit would be with me forever. Each succeeding day it was like the blanket of pain I had carried that year ebbed gently away until I was left with only loving memories.

I had been unburdened from that type of heart-parching grief until Lacey's conviction. Ever since the moment the guilty verdict was pronounced, I had felt bludgeoned by a massive club. Darkness had descended. I only functioned when I had to, and often went back to bed if no one was home. There were times I felt all the insecurities of a child. What were people saying about me behind my back? What were they thinking? Most of the time, I felt incapable of accomplishing even the simplest of goals. My mind circled like the string on a yo-yo as I grappled for coherent thought, only to see it plunge into the depths, wasted and unused. My soul was weary. I cried at nothing and everything. I prayed to God to ease my anguish. I prayed to be able to function normally. I prayed that my family would be safe, protected, and blessed. I prayed to believe again in His goodness.

Every day there were reminders that Lacey was in prison. Phone calls and emails from her, her children's sadness, the fact that the life we knew had been torched with my daughter's conviction. To try to accomplish my daily duties, I built armored walls around my heart and secured blinders around my senses to keep the pain away. *Please, Lord, guide me on this new path.*

There is a family portrait in my dining alcove of my dad and mom, my sister's family, and Ron and me with our girls. In the photo, Lacey and Trilby are the same age as Blaine and Meri were when they moved in with us. I search the picture for clues to what our life would go on to become. I find none. Smiles abound. Mom is wearing her signature blue blouse with a hummingbird pin on her lapel. Ron's hair is dark. Mine is long and layered. Lacey is wearing her red Sally Jessy Raphael glasses we bought her for her eighth-grade graduation. One hour after this photo was taken, Trilby would be kicked in the face by our colt and require stitches. In five years, Mom's breast cancer would end her life. Twenty years later, Lacey would be in prison.

My anguish dissolved so slowly I wasn't aware it was happening. One morning my soul nudged me to go outside to be in nature like I used to love to do.

Spring bulbs of purple crocus and yellow daffodils had emerged through the pliable earth. As I stepped onto my back deck, the sun above the mountain ridge showered light upon my face. Soaking in its warm radiance, I stepped forward so my entire body was bathed in its glow. I leaned into the sun's magnificence in unison with the golden daffodils. My scorched heart began to heal. The blinders I had secured so tightly around my vision began to dissipate. I'd forgotten how nurturing nature could be. A monarch butterfly, its delicate wings outlined in black, flitted from flower to flower. My heart opened wider.

For me, nature is God's canvas of love. I believe I had consciously not sought out its beauty for fear that He would not avail it to me. I had questioned His goodness when the guilty verdict was brought down on Lacey and felt forgotten by Him. I had continued to pray, but I'm not sure I'd believed He would listen. On the deck that morning, with the beauty of nature surrounding me, it was as if God was reassuring me that He was still here.

chapter 36

On Father's Day weekend, I boarded a flight to Phoenix to visit my dad. Typically when I fly, I read a book or pretend to nap so I don't have to carry on a conversation with my seatmate. That morning, however, I intended to interact with and pay attention to those around me. I was trying to remove the remainder of my blinders.

The woman in the seat next to me was about my age and was a motivational speaker. Her card read, DREAM BUILDER. She helped people create a dream-filled life. Her enthusiasm and fervor for her work captivated me. Her vitality and deep love of the life she led was inspirational. When she asked me what I did, I said I was a restaurateur and a grandmother. I didn't offer any information about Lacey because I was sure I would start crying.

Upon returning home, I signed up for my seatmate's daily inspirational emails. One message on her website was: *Some people live their lifetime the same, day in and day out, while others live each day filled with new and exciting possibilities.*

That finite message sent me into a tailspin. I had lived my days, even before Lacey's conviction, the same over and over. I got up, brewed coffee, cooked breakfast, went to work, came home, fixed dinner, watched TV, and went to bed. Nothing enticed me to do anything differently. I had no desire to seek exciting possibilities. From day to day, year to year, I only reacted to what happened in my life.

It dismantled me to view my life that way. In my advanced years, I hadn't considered what I might personally enjoy. The idea consumed me. When I thought about what dreams I wanted to fulfill, I drew a blank. What *did* I want out of life? The lady from the plane was presenting a seminar in LA that month that still had a few open seats.

I broached the idea to Ron as we refilled our morning coffee cups.

"Hon, I'm not sure I know what I'm looking for, but I feel pulled to attend this dream-building seminar." I had already told him about the woman I'd sat next to on the plane. "Are you free to watch the grandkids the days I'd be gone?"

His cup paused midway to his mouth, and he set it hard on the kitchen counter. "What are you trying to find, Bonnie? Isn't our life enough for you?"

We had been married forty years at this point, and by me putting *my* life under a microscope filtered down to *our* life also.

"I'm not sure what I'll find, honey, but I want to attend this. I need to do something for myself, and this is speaking loudly to me." I stretched up on my tiptoes and kissed him lightly on the lips. "Some people come out of her seminars with new dreams, new goals, and a new purpose in life." I rubbed my outspread fingers over his broad chest like I was polishing a genie's lamp. "I need to do this for me."

\When I arrived in Los Angeles, I was surprised by how many folks were in attendance—close to nine hundred people from all walks of life. Some were dressed in austere business suits, others in comfortable yoga pants. There were the artistic people in gauzy flowered shirts and a few, like me, in casual attire of capris and flip-flops. The age range ran the gamut from early twenties to folks older than me, judging by their gray hair and wrinkles.

It felt wonderful to be anonymous in a crowd. We proceeded through the well-orchestrated check-in and received name badges, schedules for the three days, and inspirational quotes.

During the first gathering that day, I gave myself permission to find the child within me, and to participate fully in the questionnaire. As I searched my childhood memories and wishes, I became energized—though I was also a blathering, weepy woman during some of the exercises:

- What brought you joy as a child? *Water. Family times on the lake. Reading.* (I devoured the *Nancy Drew* series.) *Writing poems and short stories. Being outside in nature.*
- What was a childhood dream? *To become a writer.*
- What goal do you set for yourself today? *To write a book that will help my grandkids.* (That answer surprised me, but I was committed to writing down the first thought that came to mind.)
- Why do you think you can do that? (My hesitant brain balked at that question, then the light bulb came on when I remembered: I had already written a book. A romance novel. I had even sent it off to Harlequin Books and Silhouette. The rejection letters I received—and life, I suppose—had stopped me writing halfway into my second novel. I had forgotten, until now, how much I had enjoyed writing.)

- What do you see yourself doing in one year? *Writing*
- If you could change one thing in your life, what would it be? *Lacey's situation.*

A shiver ran down my spine. Then my pen took on a life of its own, and my thoughts erupted onto the page. If I had been a better mother, this wouldn't have happened. Yes, my daughter was in prison, but that wasn't the excruciating pain I felt deep within. My soul knew that I had lacked as a mother. There. I said it. I had not been mentally present when my girls were young. We did lots of activities with other families, but the adults and kids were often separate. My ego had been wrapped up in making sure my family appeared perfect to the outside world. I wanted my daughters to be above reproach. Had I ever just enjoyed their company? Had I so burdened them with my fears and worries of perfection that I had made Lacey needy? Had I not shown enough love and interest in her life, leading her to crave it from others even when they had done her wrong? My writing created more disquiet than answers.

At the end of the first day, I was emotionally drained, yet I ventured onto a trolley car and headed to the ocean, hoping the calming expanse of the water would ease my troubled thoughts. In the past, when I'd stayed in strange cities for tax seminars for my accounting business, I'd always locked myself in my motel room in the evening and not emerged until morning. I would tell myself that I just wanted to read a book, when in fact I was fearful of going out alone.

On the trolley, a Jamaican woman sat next to me and giggled excitedly about how she was going to run into the ocean. Hmmm. I was just going to walk the pier, listen to the waves, and smell the salty air. When we disembarked, I watched my trolley mate run gleefully into the water. With her arms fully extended, she twirled about, tossed her head back, and laughed out loud. Feeling her joy, I decided toes-in-the-water was what I also needed. Removing my flip-flops, I rolled up my capris and relished the pliable sand between my toes. Gentle waves rose to my knees and retreated, foamy, back unto themselves. I was on a beach in California! I was ecstatic that I had followed my heart to LA, and to this ocean. It was as if each wave softened the edges of my remorse and washed away years of ho-hum, daily, un-purposed life.

The profile selfie I took that evening shows a deserted beach with a pier running into the overcast horizon, and me with a smile of contentment as I look out to sea. It's as if I knew the future would now hold better times. As I heeded the lulling sound of the waves, I vowed to remain connected to my inner child and remember what it felt like to be happy.

When I returned home, Ron immediately left to spend time at the cabin. His avoidance sabotaged my excitement. I wanted to share my experience with him, but he left the house like a man fleeing a burning building. My friend Dena told me he was worried I would leave on some dream-seeking adventure. Or, even worse, not need him anymore.

Had I found what I was looking for in LA? Yes. I'd found hope. Watching the perpetual waves on the beach, I'd realized that I was still alive, and that even with Lacey locked away, I could again experience joy.

I've read about families that fall apart after a tragic accident or life-altering event. I understand how that happens. We deal with pain and the changes in our lives differently. My family had been torn asunder when Lacey was sentenced to life in prison. I was coping the best I knew how.

My prayers for help had been answered when God's synchronicity guided me to the dream-building event. By answering those questions they'd presented me with, I had reconnected with my childhood dreams and been reminded that inner joy was what I sought. I was blessed with delight and happiness when I was surrounded by my grandkids. I loved teaching them new things and watching them experience new activities. But that was external gaiety. I yearned to find happiness inside of me, to be able to dive into my own soul and be okay with what I discovered.

part 3

chapter 37

I received my first lesson in positive thinking from my dad. At eleven years old, I wanted to dive into the pool like the cool kids. Dad went with me to the family swim hour and brought me to the edge of the pool in the deep end, where he kneeled on one knee, extended his arms over his head, placed one hand over the other, and dove artfully into the pool.

I emulated his starting position.

"Now lean over farther, Bonnie," he coached me, "and allow your hands to go into the water, then let your body glide in after."

I tried earnestly, but with each attempt, at the last minute, I'd balk and end up jumping in feet first. "I can't, Dad, I just can't," I cried.

My father was patient, but eventually, we both knew it wasn't going to happen that night. I shivered inside my blue-striped beach towel as we drove home.

Dad was silent until we pulled into our driveway. Then he turned to me. "Bonnie, tonight before you go to sleep, I want you to picture yourself in a dive position. You will gently dip your fingers into the pool, lean forward, and imagine your body and legs gliding smoothly into the water after them."

That night, I dreamt of diving. I saw my body sleek and adept, diving gracefully into the pool. The next evening, with Dad, I walked up to the edge of the deep end, bent one knee, leaned over, and splashed head-first into the water. It wasn't nearly as elegant as I'd dreamt, but the fundamental principle was there. The dreaming and the positive thinking worked. With practice, I advanced my dive to the point of being proud of how I looked when my body sliced into the water.

Perusing my bookshelf for something new to read, I came across several spiritual self-help books that I had purchased long before Lacey was arrested. It's my nature when I visit a big-city bookstore to load my arms with titles that my soul gravitates toward. Sometimes years pass before I am drawn to actually read them.

Was that the universe laying a foundation to assist me in troubled times? Was God's plan for me in this lifetime to learn to seek help from others and trust that He would provide? If so, Lacey's conviction was a tough-love way to go about it. In one of the books, the author writes that we each come into our lives with a contract and that we have agreed to overcome a trait we failed to rise above in a prior lifetime. I must have been severely deficient in a previous life to have been given this tenfold lesson.

I often wonder if the reason I drifted in my fifty-plus years was so I would be available to piece the shards of brokenness back together for Lacey and her children. Is Lacey's life journey to remain in prison for life? What about Trilby, the grandkids, and the grandparents? Did they all previously agree to partake in the fallout from Lacey's conviction? What about Selena's family? This line of thought has so many threads it seems inconceivable that every life we touch has assented to be part of our journey. Part of God's plan. Part of the big picture of the universe. The expansive ramifications are mind-boggling.

The threads in the books I read after Lacey's conviction were the power of prayer, the power of intention, and the power of positive thinking. I so wanted my prayers, my positive thinking, and my intentions to be the vehicles that won Lacey her freedom. Then I worried that God would be angry with me for not restraining myself to prayer alone. Would there be holy repercussions to my seeking alternative guidance with positive thoughts and intentions? How could I reconcile my faith in Him with my concept of positive thinking and belief that the universe was listening when I asked? Wasn't the universe God's creation? Wasn't my mom an angel up there in His heaven? Didn't all positive things come through Him?

A few months after my trip to LA, while I was sitting on my front porch, a hummingbird flew near me, dipped its wings, and hovered, flitting back and forth. The early-morning sun cast the delicate creature's shadow onto the house. As they danced in unison, a calm enveloped me. It was like my mom was saying, *"I'm here, Bonnie. I'm with you."*

She flew over to the flowerbed, and I could see her shadow on the wall; it seemed apart from her. Was she telling me to separate from the pain? Disengage from the doubt?

Dewdrops shimmered on blades of grass. A red-breasted robin hopped about the yard for insects and worms. A deer, a small two-point buck, stepped onto the lawn. He had only one antler on his left side. The right side was deformed or missing. *Even in nature, not all is perfect.* The robin pulled a worm from the ground, chortled, and flew away over the house, no doubt carrying it to her waiting babies. *Take care of those you love.* The birch leaves vibrated in the breeze, creating drumbeats for the calls of the myriad songbirds. It had rained for several days, and the forecast was for sunny skies and warmer temperatures. *You have weathered the storm.* The hummingbird feeder was full of homemade nectar and created an hourglass shadow on the porch. *It's time to heal.* The petunias and yellow snapdragons reached for the sun. The purple sage was in its early bloom. Mother Nature was giving me a beautiful morning wake-up call.

More books appeared in my stratosphere. Dena shared one she liked. It was a primer to changing your life by changing your thoughts: *Fast Food for the Soul*, by Barbara Berger. I also came across a Facebook post raving about a book by Boni Lonnsburry, *The Map To Our Responsive Universe: Where Dreams Really Do Come True.* It became my guidebook to writing down my intentions, prayers, and goals.

In my search for spiritual enlightenment, I visited an energy healer who used a light-beam generator to detox my lymphatic system. As I lay on her table, she placed large copper rings over my body to get rid of stagnant energy. My body relaxed as if I'd been given a tranquilizer. As she moved her palm over each chakra point, raising and lowering her arm above the individual energy centers, I felt a tingling.

Unsurprisingly, my heart and throat chakras were both depleted. My heart energy had closed off after Lacey's conviction, and holding my feelings in was strangling my throat. It's a mystery to me how this woman balances energy, but after one visit I felt such relief that I encouraged Ron to visit her. I believe Lacey's incarceration hit him more ruthlessly than it did me.

He visited her once, but said it was too airy-fairy for him. I also had Blaine and Meri's energies balanced, but they thought grandma was getting a little far out there with her spiritual healing.

I look back on a meditative yoga class that Dena and I attended a month before Lacey was arrested. We were instructed to become the tree we felt most attuned to while we absorbed the vibrations of the kettledrums and the crystal bowls. In the candlelit room, I unraveled from my seated position and grew into a tall, sturdy oak. My feet attached firmly to the ground, my legs became stout and robust, and my ribcage inflated as I reached my arms up and out, ever stretching and extending. My fingers spread and grew vibrant green leaves. As I stood proudly, I peeked at the other participants. Some were bent over like willows, some still scrunched on the ground like shrubs. Was God sending me a message, even back then, to believe in my own strength?

My dream-building intention of beginning to write within a year was fulfilled when I attended my first writing retreat. In a cottage named Fir, nestled among towering cedar trees and warmed by a wood-burning stove, my mind purged its painful memories onto the page. It was as if every heartsick moment of Lacey's arrest, bail time, and trial wanted to be exorcised. They became the impetus for this book.

On the last morning, I opened my "Jesus Calling" devotional by Sarah Young. Lacey and I were jointly reading the daily passages. That day's message: *I am speaking in the depths of your being. Be still, so that you can hear My voice. I speak the language of Love; My words fill you with Life and Peace, Joy and Hope.*

This time, when I arrived home, Ron greeted me with a huge hug and a kiss. "How was your week away?" he asked. Before I had left, we had agreed to be more receptive to each other's feelings.

"Oh, honey, it was glorious!" The joy of the retreat bubbled up inside of me. "Being able to share pages with other writers and talk shop . . . oh, I have so much to learn, but I feel like I've embarked on something meaningful." I was practically bouncing on the tips of my toes with excitement. "Thanks for holding down the fort."

Ron hugged me again, then held me at arm's length. "Bonnie, there's something different about you. In a good way, I mean."

"I feel different, honey."

When I shared my experience of the retreat with my friends, they marveled at my enthusiasm for writing. They said they hadn't heard my voice vibrate with that level of happiness since long before Lacey's arrest.

In the years since that retreat, I have attended various writing workshops and connected with a community of writers willing to help me hone my craft. Their reciprocity, kindness, and friendship make my heart glow, and I thank God often for their participation in my journey.

chapter 38

Dear Lacey,

This five-year anniversary is not one I would have ever dreamed of commemorating. But here goes: I want to tell you how proud I am of you and your faith in God. I'm proud that you held your head up and persevered while out on bail and continue to be a good Mom to Blaine and Meri. In court, you tried to stay positive, and I am very proud to call you my daughter. I love you so much, sweetie. I know this time apart is torturous for you. I continue to be in awe of your strength of spirit. Yes, I know it slumps occasionally, but whose doesn't? Because of the situation you found yourself in, I have been blessed with a daughter who has come to know God. I will cherish that always. Your newfound faith has kept mine intact. Thank you for that. You are forever in my heart and my thoughts. I love you. Mom

Shortly after I wrote that email, Lacey's state appeal was denied. Dispirited, she sent me information from the prison network paper on a firm that advertised post-conviction appeals and habeas corpus petitions. Researching them on Lacey's behalf, I emailed the founder, who called me the following day. He was a talker, super enthusiastic, and he shocked me when he asked the one question no one had ever asked me: "Is Lacey innocent?"

Without hesitation, I answered, "Yes."

The California firm requested a copy of all the documents pertinent to Lacey's case. As I gathered the plastic totes containing the "murder books"—that's what Haney had called the large binders filled with deputy's statements, witness statements, crime scene photos, and trial transcripts—I felt hopeful that I might uncover a flaw that could be the basis for a new appeal. Time had distanced me from the actual event, and I felt able to review and research the documentation with a detachment that would have been impossible years earlier. I accepted this as God guiding my way.

It took me over a week to sort through the papers on the makeshift plywood tabletops Ron had set up for me in his shop. Processing chronologically across my workstation, I set aside any duplicate pages to lessen the number of copies I would need to make. Yellow Post-it notes with bold titles kept my stacks organized. On a brand-new legal pad, I outlined the relevant information I wanted to highlight for the California firm. I spent hours reading all of it, hoping to find the one detail or misstep that might exonerate Lacey. My mind lived and breathed every word of every new report or statement I came across.

Hunkered down on a milk crate in the middle of the piles of paper chaos, I read the deputies' statements and the investigative notes about her case. I now understood how they had arrived at believing Lacey was guilty. It's like watching an episode of NCIS where some of the facts lean toward one person when in fact someone else has committed the crime. Information in one of the statements told of Carly putting a hit out on her taxman and how she had also sent someone to quiet Lacey. Shivers skittered through me as I remembered the thug in the blue van who had scoped out our property.

There seemed to be a thread of evidence that several druggies had snitched in exchange for the charges against them being dropped. One statement revealed that Danny had been three controlled buys away from being arrested. That led me to believe that Selena was snitching, and Carly and her drug lords were going to be implicated. Carly needed Selena silenced. Lacey fit nicely into the picture as the scorned wife. The sheriff's department saw the case as a slam dunk against Lacey and hadn't looked elsewhere.

In the bottom of the last tote I opened, after sorting and reading for several days, I found discs that contained most of the information that was in the murder books. I would only need to copy paperwork that wasn't on the CDs. I put all the information together, and mailed it off.

When the California firm was done analyzing the data, I received a call from the founder. I sat in my car in the Walmart parking lot and listened.

"I believe your daughter has a strong case for an innocence appeal," he said, his amplified voice coming through the speaker of my Bluetooth device loud and clear. "There is no evidence that proves she committed or was an accomplice to the murder. It's all circumstantial."

Yes! Finally, someone else understands. Thank You, Lord. I wasn't able to get a word in as his voice grew more excited. He named all the players involved that had led to Selena's murder, and I was impressed by his acumen regarding the case and his ability to succinctly sum it up in a conclusion of innocence.

Via prison emails and collect calls, the California firm and Lacey reviewed the details, including which legal precedents to cite, over the ensuing weeks. I was merely the secretary who assisted in gathering documents.

Months went by. Lacey and I remained optimistic that we would soon have a completed Actual Innocence Claim via Writ of Habeas Corpus to file.

chapter 39

A TV reporter contacted Lacey and said she was developing a documentary on Lacey's story for the Oxygen Channel. "I have already contacted the prosecution to tell their side," she said in an email, "but I want you to be able to tell your side of the story too. Several of our reported stories have gained the attention of the Innocence Project, and inmates have won their freedom."

The Innocence Project is a nonprofit legal organization committed to exonerating wrongly convicted people through the use of DNA testing and to reforming the criminal justice system to prevent future injustice. Lacey's case hadn't revolved around DNA evidence, but when she had arrived at the prison, she'd written them a letter, asking them to review her case. I'm not sure if they ever answered.

Lacey called me right away. She was excited at the possibility of garnering the Innocence Project's attention. However, she was also distraught that her story would be broadcast nationwide. We had survived the headlines in the local paper. Googling the reporter's name, I researched her and the Oxygen Channel. It seemed there was a multitude of TV series that exploited crime stories. *Making a Murderer* had recently received enormous attention. Other series were *Crime Couples* and *Snapped*. The one they were putting Lacey's story on was *She Made Me Do It*. The title made me queasy.

I called the California firm to get their advice about Lacey corresponding with the reporter. "Absolutely not!" he said. He also told me to contact all of Lacey's family and friends to let them know the reporter might reach out to them. "Tell them to just say, 'No comment,' and hang up the phone."

I was a bit surprised by his vehemence concerning the reporter, but I soon learned the reason for it when she called our home phone. Thankfully I, and not Blaine or Meri, was the one who answered.

The lady was all sweet and professional at first, but when I told her neither Lacey nor I would be talking with her, she became pushy. "I can't believe you won't give your daughter a chance to tell her side of the story," she said. "I'd think you would jump at an opportunity to bring television coverage and attention to her case."

I slammed the phone down. *How dare she intimate I'm not doing all I can for Lacey?* The phone rang again, and I let it go to voice mail.

"I really think you should allow us to tell Lacey's side of the story," the reporter wheedled on the message. "We've already got several people from the other side that we will be airing."

I reached for the receiver, thinking maybe I should give her Lacey's side, but then I remembered how Lacey's words had been twisted against her at trial, and I dropped my hand. I disconnected the landline from the wall and headed out the door to my car. I was behind schedule to be at our larger restaurant.

My cell phone rang before I was out of the garage and I answered it without looking. It was the reporter again. How had she gotten my cell phone number? "No comment,"

I shouted and pressed the end button. My hands shook as I texted Ron and Trilby to warn them.

When I entered the restaurant and walked into my office, the business phone rang. One of my long-term employees answered and handed the phone to me. "Someone is asking questions about Lacey."

Grabbing the receiver, I screamed into it. "There will be no comments from me, my staff, or my family. DO NOT CALL HERE AGAIN!" This lady had balls. I scribbled a note with a black marker and hung it near the phone that read: *If a caller asks about Lacey, say NO COMMENT and hang up.*

My cell phone rang again, this time from a different number. The lady would not give up. She called at various periods of the day and used different caller IDs. Now I understood why the California firm had instructed us to not say anything.

⤙＊＊＊＋

We heard through the grapevine that The Oxygen Channel was offering free airfare and a stipend of $500 to anyone who agreed to be on the show. Several of Danny's friends had been approached. The protective cage I had joyously opened after the dream-building seminar rattled closed again in my fear of what the show might cultivate. Without Lacey's depiction of the events, would the show paint her in a worse light than the newspapers had? Would this new scrutiny of Lacey's arrest and conviction hinder her appeal?

I went into prayer mode: *Dear Lord, guide the producers to show a balanced view of Lacey's case. Help keep any adverse repercussions away from our family. Please allow something good to come out of this broadcast.*

One of Lacey's friends messaged me on Facebook with a link to the trailer for the show. Watching just the advertising for it, a sickening feeling overcame me. I searched the channels for the time slot referenced in the article, and when I saw *She Made Me Do It: Lacey Hirst-Pavek* on the giant screen, I felt again like I was being slammed up against the same wall as when Lacey's mug shot first appeared on the Spokane news. Would it ever stop?

— * — * — * — +

I was hyper-vigilant the evening the show was to air and made sure the TV was off so neither Blaine or Meri would see it. I had set the recording timer at the cabin so I could go up there to view it alone. Leading up to the broadcast, the comments on the Facebook page of the local newspaper became hyped with what I believed was excitement about more dirt on our family being dragged out.

When I arrived at the cabin the next morning, the lake was calm, and mud daubers were building nests under the cabin eves. Such a peaceful scene outside, while inside, I watched the story of my daughter—produced by strangers.

The show began with a simulation of our family on a picnic in an idyllic setting like you would see in a Hallmark movie. It then went on to give a narrative about Lacey from a woman who had been no more than an acquaintance many years before. In her words, the Hirst family owned most of our small town and Lacey had been spoiled her entire life. Matt and the prosecutor were both interviewed. Their on-screen appearance irked me. Why should taxpayers pay for them to have their fifteen minutes of fame? They at least appeared uncomfortable on camera. And one remark from the prosecutor elevated my lagging spirits: "Lacey's case was largely circumstantial."

Thank You, Lord, for making sure this acknowledgment was recorded on national TV.

Rewinding the DVR, I viewed the show a second time—this time as if I were Lacey, trying to anticipate what she would take from it. The third time, I pretended I was someone who had never heard about Lacey's case. When I had researched the crime story of *Making a Murderer*, I'd seen many judgmental posts from people who had never been dealt the blow our family had suffered. I prayed Lacey's story wouldn't receive those kinds of trolling remarks.

Lacey called as I was about to push play for a fourth time. It had aired on the prison TV. Most inmates aren't aware of the intimate details of each other's crimes, and Lacey was concerned that now that her story was out, she might receive flak from the other inmates.

Thankfully, this proved not to be the case.

I felt God guiding the responses—or, rather, non-response—to Lacey and the show in the weeks that followed. He had answered my prayers, and the trolls had not opined. All the hype and anticipation in the comments before the show dwindled into remarks like, "That was it?" "Who was that girl who talked crap about Lacey?" "The Hirsts don't own the town. What else in this story was fabricated?"

Thank You, Lord, for helping us weather this storm.

chapter 40

Reflecting on the highs and lows of our journey, I see blessings in the midst. I feel favored that Lacey accepted God into her life and has shared her faith with many people. One of Lacey's out-of-town friends sent an email at one point: *Lacey, this may not even be about you. You may be a pawn for God to help touch someone else's life that he wouldn't have had access to.*

In a way, what she wrote gives me peace, but it's so difficult for me to accept Lacey's life sentence. We have now passed the six-year anniversary of her incarceration and are closing in on the seventh. Sometimes I think it should be less arduous being apart from Lacey, and that I'll eventually come to grips with her being locked away. Other times I know that will never happen. Still, I appreciate that we get phone calls from her, and can connect with her through prison email and snail mail as well.

Lacey is currently housed in the medium-security unit of the prison. God has answered my prayers and supplied her with a Christian roommate. Many of the women in her group believe in God. She has access to the law library, so she's able to keep attuned to changes in legal statutes, and there's also a Chapel library at the prison that she can turn to for inspiration.

Her visiting hours are less restrictive now, and we visit her several times a year. Each time we exit the prison doors without her, it wrenches my heart. I brood over when she will win an appeal and be released.

⚯

Rarely a day goes by that I don't thank God for my blessings. We were blessed to be able to raise Lacey's children. Blaine's senior picture depicts a healthy, handsome almost-man with piercing blue eyes that devour the camera. His serious face reveals his contemplative side as he leans against a tree in a lush grove. He is confident and self-assured and has been employed as a wild land firefighter for the past three years.

Meri is a senior now, and has the same exuberance for life her mom had at that age. A boldness radiates from the tilt of her head and her confident stance. Her pictures show a strikingly beautiful young woman with highlighted brown hair, dazzling blue eyes that radiate spunk, and skin that has an iridescent and healthy glow. She works after school as a barista at a local coffee shop.

Trilby and her family are well. My life was filled with more abundance when Trilby gave birth to our fourth grandchild. Mia Jade further infused my heart with the deep love only a grandmother understands. I feel doubly blessed to have Trilby's children in my life on an almost daily basis. I give thanks for her management skills at our larger restaurant, and I find myself looking forward to retiring altogether.

Our bubble continues to bless us with their friendship and love. My world was forever changed when God guided me to ask for their help. Because we shared that pivotal period in our lives, our friendships have been solidified with compassion. During Lacey's bail time, many from our bubble were going through drastic health issues, and our group gathered around those in need time and time again. I felt blessed to have been in their nurturing care, and to have been able to assist them in return.

The well-wishing cards we received and the good-hearted people who contacted us during Lacey's ordeal were like manna from heaven. Every kindly nod and friendly wave touched my heart and helped me feel less alone.

Ron and I recently celebrated our forty-fifth wedding anniversary. I feel incredibly blessed that our marriage survived Lacey's conviction. Our coping mechanisms were at odds many times, but as the years progressed, our communication skills improved. We often find ourselves at the kitchen table planning our full retirement, talking about purchasing a motorhome and exploring the US. Ron has reminded me that toward the end of life, our memories are all we have. For a long time, I focused on the painful memories of Lacey's situation and allowed them to pull me into despair. I now look forward to retiring with Ron by my side and creating many happy memories into our twilight years.

Two years after the California firm started on Lacey's case, we received the legal writ that could exonerate her and free her from prison. Its premise centers on the evidence, or lack thereof, in her case.

All of our hopes for Lacey's freedom are wrapped into this thirty-page appeal. To finally receive the writ and realize this could open the door to Lacey's freedom was exhilarating, but we know it could also pave a gateway for more headlines in the paper and a rehash of all the unfortunate details of the murder. We have been told this is her last shot at freedom. I don't understand all the legal cases cited in the appeal, but the rest of it seems well explained, proposed, and followed through on with sound reasoning. I can only pray that the two-year delay in preparing it has put open judicial minds in the correct positions at the proper time.

What do I believe in now? I believe that what I pray about, God will take care of. I am surprised that I can say that. It's what I used to believe—that God would make everything work out for the best. Did He? Not to my liking, but maybe it all played out according to His plan. I've realized that I'm not privy to that plan, so I try to focus more on my blessings and seek to acknowledge the positive in all things.

chapter 41

I'm now nearing my sixty-fourth birthday. I've often pronounced that I'm going to live well past one hundred years old. But is that what I really want? Do I want to see any more sadness or death? We lost Ron's dad in September 2016. Do I want to live forty more years and endure more agony like Lacey's trial and conviction? What is God's plan for me?

I was with Ron's dad when he passed. It was my first time witnessing that last breath, the suspension of sound and the tranquility of the hereafter as he left his body. I had often wondered if I could bear witness and be a comfort to anyone in their final days, or if I would I fall back into that dark pit of pain I inhabited after Lacey's trial.

Meri was with me when her great grandpa took his last breath. I tried to shield her, but she was adamant that she wanted to be with him when he passed. She had visited Bob daily in his last few months, and they had developed a steadfast bond. I connect her need to be with him at the end to a desire to remedy the fact she was kept away from her mother's annihilation in the courtroom. This time, she didn't want the details sugarcoated, or delivered after the fact. She wanted to be there at the end.

Sometimes I wish I hadn't been there at the final moment of Lacey's trial. Escapism, I believe, is the word I search for. To negate the bad and relish the good. I have become more vested in the solace that family, friends, and nature provide in recent years. Whether I'm in my kayak on a calm lake or absorbing the power of the ocean or watching a hummingbird dance with its shadow, I accept these as God's gifts—His proof that there is hope. There is faith. There is a God.

In the eight-month span following Bob's passing, Ron's mom lingered in a near-death state for several weeks before leaving this world, and my dad was in hospice for a week before he went with his angels. I was honored to sit bedside with all of them. If there can be a blessing in death, then I'd like to believe my attendance was a blessing to them.

chapter 42

It is a brisk fall morning. As I sit on the deck at our cabin, a slight breeze dimples the lake's surface nearest me and rustles the teardrop leaves of the aspen trees. My face is cold above the afghan I am wrapped up in. The sun is poking out from the clouds. On the far side of the narrow lake, the wind has not yet touched its surface. The water there is smooth, similar to the way I see my life right now.

I am a wife, mother, grandmother, daughter, sister, and friend. These are the relationships that nurture me. They are what I treasure. My prayers now are to be like the sturdy oak. To be able to gather my loved ones under my protective branches and help them feel safe and loved.

As the breeze subsides, the unruffled illusion on the lake's surface moves toward me and beckons me into my destiny.

acknowledgments

I send love and gratitude to the multitude of teachers, writers, family, and friends who have encouraged me along the way. To Hedgebrook, The Fine Arts Work Center, and Dani Shapiro, for giving me my first taste of the writing community sisterhood. Special thanks to the private workshop group Raucous Women Still Writing and its original members, who helped fine-tune my woeful writing skills: Marci Rich, Katie Devine, Nina Boug Lichtenstein, Karen Gentry, Sharon Day, Gigi Papoulias, Laura Hoffman, Sarla Nichols, and Jessica Barlevi Halepsis.

To my husband, Ron, for understanding my need to write this story and facilitating the time for me to burrow into my pages: I am ever thankful that our love survived.

To my daughter Lacey, for assisting me in memory and fact-finding so I could write the truest-to-life memoir possible: your faith and grace inspire me to be a better person. To Lacey's children, Blaine and Meri: thank you for enriching my life with your love, and for putting up with my quirky grandma ways.

To my daughter Trilby Michels: you were my rock in this tumultuous time. Thank you for always bringing me back to center and for sharing your daughters, Rylee and Mia, with me. Their youthful enthusiasm kept me grounded.

To my sister Pat Coderre: blessings to you for being the best big sis a girl could have. Your unending emotional support and love is a godsend.

To the multitude of workshop teachers and fellow students I've learned from and written alongside: thank you for your critiques of my pages. This book is a testament to the wonderment of writing communities. A special thank-you to Andre Dubus III; your encouragement to complete my pages for myself and for Lacey was the impetus I sorely needed at the time. To Laura Munson: thank you for your continued enthusiasm and support. To Andrea Jarrell and Jennifer Haupt: from the beginning of my writing journey, you have been my inspiration. To my beta readers, Tayna Mozias Slavin, Pamela Lorenz, and Lacey Hirst-Pavek: thank you for your honest insights. Thanks to Marion Roach Smith for her magical structural editing, and Rob Brill for his copyedits. To Brooke Warner, Krissa Lagos, and Cait Levin of She Writes Press for making my book shine.

To our bubble—Al and Nanc Murphy, Steve and Dena Byl, Elaine Hamilton, Guy and Sherise Layton, Bob Henrie, Doug and Becky Patrick, Don Weyer, Stacey Woodward, Randy Hirst—your support on those hard benches and in our everyday life was a blessing from heaven. A mere thanks isn't enough to convey the positive impact you've had on my heart.

To my parents, Harold and Evelyn Snively: Thank you for being my example of a faith-based life. May you continue to guide my realm of guardian angels as they watch over me.

about the author

B onnie S. Hirst loves feel-good movies and stories with happy endings. After a thirty-five-year hiatus from writing (during which time she was busy being a mom and grandma), she is enjoying connecting with other writers. When life tries to shorten her stride, she prays, cries, talks with her guardian angels, reads self-help books, and writes. She can often be found kayaking on a calm mountain lake. Connect with her on Facebook: https://www.facebook.com/BonnieSHirst.

Author photo © Chris Loomis

SELECTED TITLES FROM SHE WRITES PRESS

She Writes Press is an independent publishing company founded to serve women writers everywhere. Visit us at www.shewritespress.com.

Rethinking Possible: A Memoir of Resilience by Rebecca Faye Smith Galli. $16.95, 978-1-63152-220-8. After her brother's devastatingly young death tears her world apart, Becky Galli embarks upon a quest to recreate the sense of family she's lost—and learns about healing and the transformational power of love over loss along the way.

Breathe: A Memoir of Motherhood, Grief, and Family Conflict by Kelly Kittel. $16.95, 978-1-938314-78-0. A mother's heartbreaking account of losing two sons in the span of nine months—and learning, despite all the obstacles in her way, to find joy in life again.

Blinded by Hope: One Mother's Journey Through Her Son's Bipolar Illness and Addiction by Meg McGuire. $16.95, 978-1-63152-125-6. A fiercely candid memoir about one mother's roller coaster ride through doubt and denial as she attempts to save her son from substance abuse and bipolar illness.

Renewable: One Woman's Search for Simplicity, Faithfulness, and Hope by Eileen Flanagan. $16.95, 978-1-63152-968-9. At age forty-nine, Eileen Flanagan had an aching feeling that she wasn't living up to her youthful ideals or potential, so she started trying to change the world—and in doing so, she found the courage to change her life.

Of This Much I'm Sure: A Memoir by Nadine Kenney Johnstone. $16.95, 978-1631522109. After an IVF procedure leads to near-fatal internal bleeding, Nadine Kenney Johnstone must ask herself if the journey to create life is worth risking her own—and eventually learns that in an unpredictable life, the only thing she can be sure of is the healing power of hope.

A Leg to Stand On: An Amputee's Walk into Motherhood by Colleen Haggerty. $16.95, 978-1-63152-923-8. Haggerty's candid story of how she overcame the pain of losing a leg at seventeen—and of terminating two pregnancies as a young woman—and went on to become a mother, despite her fears.